Lecture Notes in Computer Science 1410
Edited by G. Goos, J. Hartmanis and J. van Leeuwen

Springer
Berlin
Heidelberg
New York
Barcelona
Hong Kong
London
Milan
Paris
Singapore
Tokyo

T.V. Raman

Audio System for Technical Readings

Springer

Series Editors

Gerhard Goos, Karlsruhe University, Germany
Juris Hartmanis, Cornell University, NY, USA
Jan van Leeuwen, Utrecht University, The Netherlands

Author

T.V. Raman
Adobe Systems, Advanced Technology Group
(W14 129) 345 Park Avenue
San Jose, CA 95110-2704, USA
E-mail: raman@adobe.com

Cataloging-in-Publication data applied for

Die Deutsche Bibliothek - CIP-Einheitsaufnahme

Raman, T. V.:
Audio system for technical readings / T. V. Raman. [Association for Computing Machinery]. - Berlin ; Heidelberg ; New York ; Barcelona ; Hong Kong ; London ; Milan ; Paris ; Singapore ; Tokyo : Springer, 1998
(Lecture notes in computer science ; 1410)
ISBN 3-540-65515-8

CR Subject Classification (1998): H.5, I.7, I.2.1

ISSN 0302-9743
ISBN 3-540-65515-8 Springer-Verlag Berlin Heidelberg New York

Typesetting: Camera-ready by author
SPIN 10637184 06/3142 – 5 4 3 2 1 0 Printed on acid-free paper

To my guiding eyes, ASTER

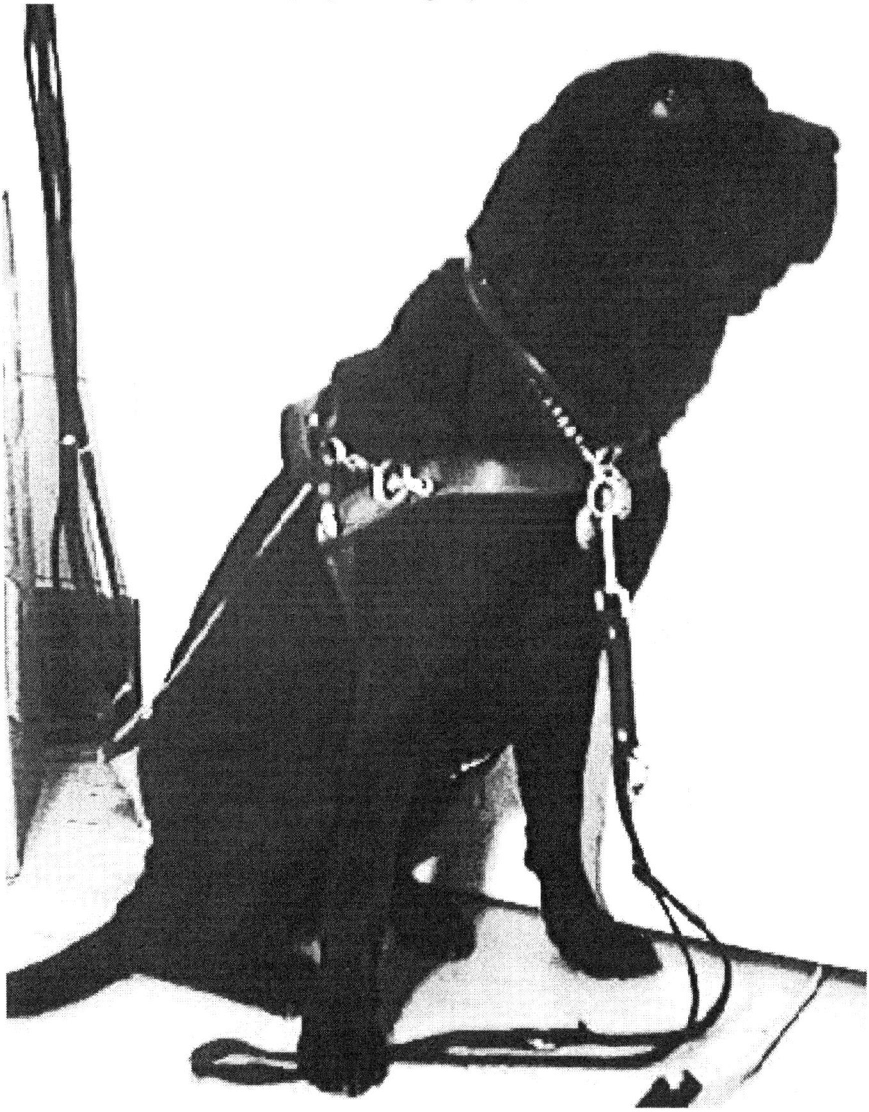

Foreword By Prof. David Gries

Once in a while, something nice happens, as if by coincidence, serendipitously. It happened to me when T.V. Raman asked me to supervise his Ph.D. thesis on building a system to speak documents, especially those with technical content or a lot of structure.

The project had many interesting points, for example: the need for a programming language for writing speaking rules (a sort of postscript for the ear instead of for paper), the need for a multi-dimensional model of speech and sound (so that the speaking-rule language could be largely independent of the particular voice synthesizer being used), knowledge of mathematics and the development of ways to speak it well, the development of a new internal form for mathematics, software engineering (in his 35,000-line CLOS program AsTeR, Raman makes ingenious use of object-oriented features of CLOS), and human-interface issues in making AsTeR interactive.

Finally, there was a real *need* for AsTeR. Previously, it was almost impossible for the visually handicapped to access technical documents. RFB (Recordings For The Blind) takes up to a year to make a recording of a technical book, and the only other way for a visually handicapped person to access a technical document is to have someone read it to them. The development of AsTeR is one more instance of the usefulness of computers.

Recordings For The Blind held a workshop-conference on AsTeR three months after the thesis was completed and will soon begin producing cassette tapes using it. Not only can a tape of a book be made in a day or two (instead of a year), but the quality is far superior to that produced by humans. In addition, Recordings For The Blind would like to make AsTeR available to the blind who are computer-literate, allowing them to make full use of AsTeR's interactive capabilities.

The applications of the concepts and technology in AsTeR are many. For one, just consider being able to call your computer on the phone and have your e-mail read to you in a comprehensible fashion. The results are so noteworthy that *SIAM News* published a column on Raman and AsTeR (March 1994, page 7).

What makes this thesis even more intriguing is that Raman himself is visually handicapped. He cannot see his keyboard or monitor. He uses a guide-dog, Aster, to help him get around. And yet, Raman did *all* the programming of system AsTeR himself. My role was that of advisor. We discussed issues, I gave him advice based on my experience, I pointed him at literature, and I helped him in editing and organizing the thesis itself and a few papers that came from it (though all the writing on the computer was done by Raman himself). The real work, however, was his alone.

Raman is one of the most courageous, up-beat, and positive people I have known. Blind, he came from India to do his PhD work in Cornell's field of applied mathematics. He acquired his guide dog, Aster, after arriving here. He studied applied math and computer science and began using computers in a big way (with a screen reader). All this without a complaint, with the most positive and optimistic attitude I have seen.

Just consider this anecdote. After his PhD, Raman accepted an offer at a major computer manufacturer. While still at Cornell, surfing the net, Raman came across a notice on a bulletin board to the following effect. Jack's (a fictitious name) job was to go to T.V.'s future department and tell them how to treat Raman (because of his handicap). Jack, however, had little real experience with such matters, and he wanted advice from whomever would give it to him —what should he tell the department? Raman came into my room laughing about it. He had replied to Jack: tell the department to treat him just the way they would treat anyone else!

AsTeR is indeed a wonderful achievement. For me, however, AsTeR was not the most important part of this endeavor. Instead, it was working daily with Raman over a two-to-three year period. Always positive, with never a complaint, brilliant in his own way, Raman was a pleasure to deal with. It is an experience I will value for years to come.

David Gries
William L. Lewis Professor of Engineering
Computer Science Department
Cornell University
Ithaca, NY

Preface

> The advent of electronic documents makes information available in more than its visual form —electronic information can now be display-independent. We describe a computing system, AsTeR, that *audio formats* electronic documents to produce audio documents.

The development of AsTeR was the basis of the author's dissertation, which was presented to the Faculty of the Graduate School of Cornell University in fulfillment of the Requirements for the Degree of Doctor of Philosophy in 1994. This preface, written three years later, puts the work in perspective with respect to the developments in the world of electronic information and auditory interfaces between 1994 and 1997. The main body of this work remains identical to what was presented in 1994.

Introduction

AsTeR was motivated by the insight that information presentation needs to take advantage of the specific perceptual modality in use. This typeset manuscript exploits features of visual interaction to convey information effectively; in the same vein, AsTeR introduced the notion of *audio formatting* to enable rich aural presentations of structured information.

Speech-enabling Applications

The insights gained from developing and using AsTeR have been applied to the more general problem of providing aural access to computer interfaces, starting in late 1994. Computer interfaces encapsulate man-machine dialogue, and once we realize that "The document *is* the interface", the technique of synthesizing effective aural presentations starting with the information instead of its visual presentation leads naturally to the speech-enabling approach —see [Ram96a, Ram96b, Ram97b]. The speech-enabling approach —a technique that separates computation from the user interface —is described in detail in [Ram97a]. Application designers can implement desired features in the computational component and have different user interfaces expose the resulting functionality in the manner most suited to a given user environment. This leads to the design of high-quality Auditory User Interfaces (AUI) that integrate speech as a first class citizen into the user interface.

Structured Information And The WWW

AsTeR pointed out the advantages to come in a world where documents are first created electronically before being turned into modality-specific presentations such as typeset documents for printing. The work also pointed out the need for such electronic information to be well-structured to enable *computation* on this information.

The last few years have seen an explosive growth in electronic information on the Internet fueled by the popularity of the WWW. The initial rush to the WWW resulted in publishers putting out rich visual content with a concomitant abuse of document structure as envisioned in AsTeR. As a consequence, content providers on the WWW today face many of the challenges outlined in AsTeR when attempting to create electronic content that can be repurposed for publishing online as well as in traditional print formats. This has also led to a vast amount of Webformation that is becoming increasingly difficult to navigate and categorize —see [Hay96, Gib96].

Faced by these challenges, content providers on the WWW are now looking to create richly tagged information using markup systems like XML. As the first such example, mathematical Markup Language (MathML) is an XML application for describing mathematical notation and capturing both its structure and content. The goal of MathML is to enable mathematics to be served, received, and processed on the Web, just as HTML has enabled this functionality for text —*URL* http://www.w3.org/TR/WD-math/.

Conclusion

As humans, we see, hear, feel and smell. Human interaction is enriched by the concomitant redundancy introduced by multimodal communication. In contrast, computer interfaces until now have relied primarily on visual interaction —today's interfaces are like the *silent* movies of the past! As we approach the turn of the century, computers now have the ability to talk, listen and perhaps, even *understand.* Integrating new modalities like speech into human-computer interaction requires rethinking how information systems are designed in today's world of *visual* computing.

Visually rich computing introduced the notion of What You See Is What You Get (WYSIWYG) documents; but by carrying it too far, we risk ending up in a world of "What You See Is All You Have" documents. On the positive side, the exponential growth in electronic information combined with a desire to be able to intelligently process this content and access it whenever, wherever and however the user chooses provides adequately strong reasons to suggest that the world will move away from the present situation of *see-only* documents.

That a blind person can navigate the Internet just as efficiently and effectively as any sighted person attests to the profound potential of digital documents to improve human communication. Printed documents are fixed snapshots of changing ideas; they limit the means of communication to the paper on which they are stored. But in electronic form, documents can become raw material for computers that can extract, catalogue and rearrange the ideas in them. Used properly, technology can separate the message from the medium so that we can access information wherever, whenever and in whatever form we want.

Archiving information in a structurally rich form will ensure that this vast repository of knowledge can be reused, searched and displayed in ways that best suit individuals' needs and abilities, using software not yet invented or even imagined.

The coming millenium is likely to prove an exciting one in the world of electronic information.

T. V. Raman

December 6, 1997 Mountain View, CA. *URL* http://cs.cornell.edu/home/raman

Acknowledgements

I thank my adviser, David Gries, for his help and guidance in turning a collection of useful ideas into a practicable thesis. His insight into defining a language for audio formatting proved crucial in realizing my ultimate goal of producing a system that does for audio documents what systems like (La)TeX have achieved in the world of printed documents. I also acknowledge the help and support of the other members of my committee, John Hopcroft, Dan Huttenlocher, Dexter Kozen, Keith Dennis and John Guckenheimer.

My former office-mate, M. S. Krishnamoorthy (RPI), was the first to spot the potential presented by my prototype, TeXTalK. He, along with John Hopcroft, Keith Dennis and Brian Kernighan (ATT), encouraged me to take up the problem of producing audio renderings from electronic markup source for my dissertation. Tim Teitelbaum and Anne Neirynck helped in the initial phase when I was defining the problem. Bruce Donald was my adviser during the first phase of the project. We had many useful discussions, and I am grateful to him for convincing me to implement my system in Lisp-CLOS. Bruce Donald and CSRVL (Computer Science Robotics and Vision Lab) supported my work with a research assistantship and equipment.

My summer experience at the Xerox Palo Alto Research Center (PARC) helped me crystalize many ideas. Dennis Arnon of Xerox PARC pointed out the importance of working with document logical structure. Xerox Corp. also supported my work with an equipment grant in spring 1992. Jim Davis (Cornell DRI) advised me on lexical choice when producing spoken mathematics, helped improve my Lisp programming skills, and also contributed some Lisp code used to communicate with the speech synthesizer.

Intel Corp. supported my work with a one-year fellowship for the academic year 1992-93 and a research grant for fall 93. I acknowledge the help and support of my Intel mentor, Murali Veeramoney, and the other members of his group. Jim Larson (Intel Architecture Labs) helped me crystalize some of my ideas on user-interface design during the many stimulating discussions we had over the summer of 1993.

I implemented AsTeR and wrote this thesis using an Intel-486 PC from CSRVL running IBM Screen Reader. I thank the Center for Applied Mathematics (CAM) for opening up the world of computing to me by acquiring an Accent speech synthesizer and IBM Screen Reader —Screen Reader, designed by Jim Thatcher (IBM Watson Research Center), is one of the most robust screen-reading programs available today. I acknowledge the support of our systems administrators for their untiring help in my efforts to adapt my setup to use the software available.

I also thank the USENET community for their support in helping configure the various pieces of software that I use. The *Emacs* editor and Screen, a public-domain window manager for ASCII terminals, have together provided a powerful computing environment that has enabled me to be fully productive. Lack of online documentation for Lisp was overcome with help from the USENET (comp.lang.lisp) community. I also thank Nelson Beebee for his invaluable help on (LA)TeX throughout the writing of this thesis. I thank the authors and publishers of the texts listed in Table B for providing me online access to the electronic sources —these proved invaluable both as online references as well as test material for AsTeR.

Taking classes at Cornell was an enjoyable experience, and I thank all the faculty for their help. Every effort was made to provide online lecture notes —AsTeR was motivated by the availability of online notes for CS681 taught by Dexter Kozen. Talking books from Recording for the Blind (RFB) proved invaluable. I was also ably assisted by a dedicated group of readers. Anindya Basu, Bill Barry (ORST), Jim Davis, Harsh Kaul and Matthai Phillipose proof-read this thesis and suggested many useful improvements. I also thank Holly Mingins, Dolores Pendell (CAM) and the rest of the administrative staff of the CS department for their help and support. I thank Bert Adams of the Cornell Physical Education program for helping me stay fit during the last four years and Mike Dillon (NYSCBVH) for orienting me around the Cornell campus.

Finally, I thank my family for their love and support throughout.

Table of Contents

1. Audio System for Technical Readings

1.1 Motivation

Documents encapsulate structured information. Visual formatting renders this structure on a two-dimensional display (paper or a video screen) using accepted conventions. The visual layout helps the reader recreate, internalize and browse the underlying structure. The ability to selectively access portions of the display, combined with the layout, enables multiple views. For example, a reader can first skim a document to obtain a high-level view and then read portions of it in detail.

The rendering is attuned to the visual mode of communication, which is characterized by the spatial nature of the display and the eye's ability to actively access parts of this display. The reader is active, while the rendering itself is passive.

This active-passive role is reversed in oral communication: information flows actively past a passive listener. This is particularly evident in traditional forms of reproducing audio, e.g., cassette tapes. Here, a listener can only browse the audio with respect to the underlying time-line —by rewinding or forwarding the tape. The passive nature of listening prohibits multiple views —it is impossible to first obtain a high-level view and then "look" at portions of the information in detail.

Traditionally, documents have been made available in audio by trained readers speaking the contents onto a cassette tape to produce "talking books". Being non-interactive, these do not permit browsing. They do have the advantage that the reader can interpret the information and convey a particular view of the structure to the listener. However, the listener is restricted to the single view present on the tape. In the early 80's, text-to-speech technology was combined with OCR (Optical Character Recognition) to produce "reading machines". In addition to being non-interactive, renderings produced from scanning visually formatted text convey very little structure. Thus, the true audio document was non-existent when we started our work.

We overcome these problems of oral communication by developing the notion of *audio formatting* —and a computing system that implements it. Audio formatting renders information structure orally, using speech augmented by non-speech sound cues. The renderings produced by this process are attuned to an auditory display —*audio layout* present in the output conveys information structure. Multiple audio views are enabled by making the renderings interactive. A listener can change how specific information structures are rendered and browse them selectively. Thus, the listener becomes an active participant in oral communication.

In the past, information was available only in a visual form, and it required a human to recreate its inherent structure. Electronic information has opened a new world: Information can now be captured in a display-independent manner —using, e.g., tools like SGML[1] and (LA)TEX[2]. Though the principal mode of display is still visual, we can now produce alternative renderings, such as oral and tactile displays. We take advantage of this to audio-format information structure present in (LA)TEX documents. The resulting *audio documents* achieve effective oral communication of structured information from a wide range of sources, including literary texts and highly technical documents containing complex mathematics.

The results of this thesis are equally applicable to producing audio renderings of structured information from such diverse sources as information databases and electronic libraries. Audio formatting clients can be developed to allow seamless access to a variety of electronic information, available on both local and remote servers. Thus, the server provides the information, and various clients, such as visual or audio formatters, provide appropriate views of the information. Our work is therefore significant in the area of developing adaptive computer technologies.

Today's computer interfaces are like the silent movies of the past! As speech becomes a more integral part of human-computer interaction, our work will become more relevant in the general area of user-interface design, by adding audio as a new dimension to computer interfaces.

1.2 What is ASTER?

ASTER is a computing system[3] for producing audio renderings of electronic documents. The present implementation works with documents written in the TEX family of markup[4] languages: TEX, LATEX and AMS-TEX. We were motivated by the need to render technical documents, and much effort was spent on designing audio renderings of complex mathematical formulae. However, ASTER works equally well on structured documents from non-technical subjects. Finally, the design of ASTER is not restricted to any single markup language —all that is needed to handle documents written in another markup language is a recognizer for it.

ASTER recognizes the logical structure of a document embodied in the markup and represents it internally. The internal representation is then ren-

[1] Standard Generalized Markup Language (SGML) captures information in a layout independent form.

[2] LATEX, designed by Leslie Lamport, is a document preparation system based on the TEX typesetting system developed by Donald Knuth.

[3] In real life, ASTER is a guide-dog, a big friendly black Labrador.

[4] To most people, *markup* means an increase in the price of an article. Here, "markup" is a term from the publishing and printing business, where it means the instructions for the typesetter, written on a typescript or manuscript copy by an editor. Typesetting systems like (LA)TEX have these commands embedded in the electronic source. A *markup language* is a set of means (constructs) to express how text (i.e., that which is not markup) should be processed, or handled in other ways.

dered in audio by applying a collection of rendering rules written in AFL, our language for audio formatting. Rendering an internalized high-level representation enables AsTeR to produce different views of the information. A user can either listen to an entire document, or browse its internal structure and listen to portions selectively. The rendering and browsing components of AsTeR can also work with high-level representations from sources such as OCR-based document recognition.

This chapter gives an overview of AsTeR, which is implemented in *Lisp-CLOS* with an *Emacs* front-end. The recommended way of using it is to run *Lisp* as a subprocess of *Emacs.* Throughout this chapter, we assume familiarity with basic *Emacs* concepts.

Section 1.3 introduces AsTeR by showing how documents can be rendered and browsed. Sec. 1.4 explains how AsTeR can be extended to render newly defined document structures in (LA)TeX. Sec. 1.5 gives some examples of changing between different ways of rendering the same information. Sec. 1.6 presents some advanced techniques that can be used when listening to complex documents such as text-books. AsTeR can render information produced by various sources. We give an example of this by demonstrating how AsTeR can be used to interact with the *Emacs* calculator, a full-fledged symbolic algebra system.

1.3 Rendering Documents

This section assumes that AsTeR has been installed and initialized — see App. A.1 for details of the software and hardware configuration. At this point, text within any file being visited in *Emacs* (in general, text in any *Emacs* buffer) can be rendered in audio. To listen to a piece of text, mark it using standard *Emacs* commands and invoke *read-aloud-region*[5]. This results in the marked text being audio formatted using a standard rendering style. The text can constitute an entire document or book; it could also be a short paragraph or a single equation from a document —AsTeR renders both partial and complete documents. This is the simplest and also the most common type of interaction with AsTeR.

The input may be plain *ASCII* text; in this case, AsTeR will recognize the minimal document structure present —e.g., paragraph breaks and quoted text. On the other hand, (LA)TeX markup helps AsTeR recognize more of the logical structure and, as a consequence, produce more sophisticated renderings.

[5] This is an *Emacs Lisp* command, and in the author's setup, it is bound to *C-z d.*

Browsing the Document

Next to getting AsTeR to speak, the most important thing is to get it to stop speaking. Audio renderings can be interrupted by executing *reader-quit-reading*[6]. The listener can then traverse the internal structure by moving the *current selection*, which represents the current position in the document (e.g., current paragraph), by executing any of the browser commands *reader-move-previous*, *reader-move-next*, *reader-move-up* or *reader-move-down*.

To orient the user within the document structure, the current selection is summarized by verbalizing a short message of the form "<*context*> is <*type*>", e.g., moving down one level from the top of the equation

$$\sum_{1<=i<=n} i = \frac{n(n+1)}{2} \tag{1.1}$$

AsTeR speaks the message "*left hand side* is *summation*". The user has the option of either listening to just the current selection (*reader-read-current*) or listening to the rest of the document (*reader-read-rest*). Chap. 5 gives a detailed overview of the browser.

Examples of Use

AsTeR can be used to:

- Read technical articles and books. The files for such documents may be available on the local system or on the global *Internet*[7]. Resources retrieved over the network can be audio formatted by AsTeR, since they are just text in *Emacs* buffers. The author has listened to this thesis as well as 10 textbooks using AsTeR. In addition, AsTeR has rendered a wide collection of technical documents available on the *INTERNET*, including technical reports and **AMS** bulletins.
- Entertain. About 200 electronic texts are available on the *INTERNET*, including the complete works of Shakespeare. The majority of these documents are in plain *ASCII*, but the quality of audio renderings produced by AsTeR, based on the minimal document structure that can be recognized, still surpasses the output of conventional reading machines. Increased availability of electronic texts marked up in (LaTeX)TeX and SGML will enable better recognition of document structure and, as a consequence, better audio renderings.
- Proof-read partial and complete documents under preparation. This feature is specially useful when typesetting complex mathematical formulae.

[6] Bound to C-b q.

[7] *ANGE-FTP*, an *Emacs* utility written by Andy Norman, allows seamless access to remote files. In addition, *Emacs* clients are available for networked information retrieval systems like *GOPHER*, *WWW* and *WAIS*.

This thesis has been proof-read using AsTeR and the system helped the author locate several minor errors, including bad punctuation. Thus, though designed as a system for rendering documents, the flexible design, combined with the power afforded by the *Emacs* editor, turns AsTeR into a very useful document preparation aid.

1.4 Extending AsTeR

The quality of audio renderings produced by AsTeR depends on how much of the document logical structure is recognized. Authors of (LA)TEX documents often use their own macros[8] to encapsulate specific logical structures. Of course, AsTeR does not initially know of these extensions. User-defined (LA)TEX macros are initially rendered in a canonical way; typically, they are spoken as they appear in the running text. Thus, given a document containing

```
$A \kronecker B$
```

AsTeR would say

cap a kronecker cap b

In this case, this canonical rendering is quite acceptable.

In general, how AsTeR renders such user-defined structures is fully customizable. The first step is to extend the recognizer to handle the new construct, in this case, `\kronecker`. Sec. 2.4 explains the principles on which such extensions are based. Here, we give the reader a brief example of how this mechanism is used in practice.

The recognizer is extended by calling *Lisp* macro *define-text-object* as follows:

```
(define-text-object :macro-name "kronecker" :number-args 0
:processing-function kronecker-expand
:object-name kronecker
:supers (binary-operator) :precedence  multiplication)
```

This extends the recognizer; instances of macro `\kronecker` are represented by object *kronecker*. The user can now define any number of renderings for instances of object *kronecker*.

AFL (see Chap. 3), our language for audio formatting, is used to define rendering rules (see Chap. 4). Here is one such rendering rule for object *kronecker*:

```
(def-reading-rule (kronecker simple)
    "Simple rendering rule for object kronecker."
  (read-aloud "kronecker product of ")
  (read-aloud (first (children kronecker)))
  (read-aloud " and ")
  (read-aloud (second (children kronecker))))
```

[8] Macros permit an author to define new language constructs in TEX and specify how these constructs should be rendered on paper.

AsTeR would now speak `$A \kronecker B$` as

kronecker product of cap a and cab b.

Notice that the order in which the elements of $A \otimes B$ are spoken is independent of the order in which they appear on paper. AsTeR derives its power from representing document content as objects and by allowing multiple user-defined rendering rules for individual object types. These rules can cause any number of audio events (ranging from speaking a simple phrase, to playing a digitized sound). Once the recognizer has been extended by an appropriate call to *define-text-object*, user-defined macros in (LA)TEX can be handled just as well as any standard (LA)TEX construct.

To give an example of this, the logo that appears on the first page of this chapter is produced by (LA)TEX macro `\asterlogo`. After extending the recognizer with an appropriate call to *define-text-object*, we can define an audio rendering rule that produces a bark when rendering instances of this macro.

1.5 Producing Different Audio Views

AsTeR can render a given object in more than one way. The listener can switch among any of several predefined renderings for a given object to produce different *views*, or add to these by defining new rendering rules.

Activating a rendering rule is the simplest way of changing how a given object is rendered. Statement

(*activate-rule* <*object-name*> <*rule-name*>)

activates rule <*rule-name*> for object <*object-name*>. Thus, executing

(*activate-rule* 'paragraph 'summarize)

activates rule *summarize* for object *paragraph*.

Suppose we wish to skip all instances of *verbatim* text in a LATEX document. We could define and activate the following *quiet* rendering rule for object *verbatim*:

```
(def-reading-rule (verbatim quiet) nil)
```

Later, to hear the *verbatim* text in a document, the previously activated rule *quiet* can be deactivated by executing

```
(deactivate-rule 'verbatim)
```

Notice that at any given time, only one rendering rule is active for any object. Hence, we need only specify the object name when deactivating a rendering rule.

Activating a new rule is a convenient way of changing how instances of a specific object are rendered. Rendering *styles* enable the user to make more global changes to the renderings. Activating style *style-1* by executing

```
(activate-style 'style-1)
```

activates rendering rule *style-1* for all objects for which this rendering rule is defined. All other objects continue to be rendered as before. This is also true when a sequence of rendering styles is successively activated. Thus, activating rendering styles is a convenient way of progressively customizing the rendering of a complex document.

The effect of activating a style can be undone at any time by executing

(*deactivate-style <style-name>*)

AsTeR provides the following rendering styles:

- *Variable-substitution*: Use variable substitution to render complex mathematical expressions —see Sec. 4.6.
- *Use-special-pattern*: Recognize special patterns in mathematical expressions to produce context-specific renderings. For example, this enables AsTeR to speak A^T as "cap a transpose".
- *Descriptive*: Produce descriptive renderings for mathematics. —see Sec. 4.5.
- *Simple*: Produce a base-level audio notation for mathematical expressions —see Sec. 4.3.
- *Default*: Produce default renderings.
- *Summarize*: Provide a summary.
- *Quiet*: Skip objects.

When AsTeR is initialized, the following styles are active, with the leftmost style being the most recently activated style.

```
(use-special-pattern descriptive simple default)
```

Defining a new rendering style is equivalent to defining a collection of rendering rules having the same name. Note that a rendering style need not provide rules for all objects in the document logical structure. As explained earlier, activating a style only affects the renderings of those objects for which the style provides a rule.

1.6 Using the Full Power of AsTeR

This section demonstrates some advanced features of AsTeR that are useful when rendering complex documents. AsTeR recognizes cross-references and allows the listener to traverse these as hypertext links. Cross-referenceable objects can be labeled interactively, and these labels can be used when referring to such objects within renderings. The ability to switch among rendering rules enables multiple views and allows the listener to quickly locate portions of interest in a document. By activating rendering rules, all instances of a particular object can be floated to the end of the containing hierarchical unit, e.g., all footnotes can be floated to the end of a paragraph. This is convenient when getting a quick overview of a document. AsTeR also provides a simple bookmark facility for marking positions of interest to be returned to later. Finally, AsTeR can be interfaced with sources of structured information other than electronic documents. Later, we demonstrate this by interfacing AsTeR to the *Emacs* calculator.

Cross-References

Cross-reference tags that occur in the body of a document are represented internally as instances of object *cross-reference* and contain a link to the object being referenced. Of course, how such cross-reference tags are rendered depends on the currently active rule for object *cross-reference.* The default rendering rule for cross-references presents the user with a summary of the object being cross-referenced, e.g., the number and title of a sectional unit. This is followed by a non-speech audio prompt. Pressing a key at this prompt results in the entire cross-referenced object being rendered at this point — rendering continues if no key is pressed within a certain time interval. In addition, the listener can interrupt the rendering and move through the cross-reference tags. This is useful in cases where many such tags occur within the same sentence.

Labeling a Cross-Referenceable Object

Consider a proof that reads:

> By theorem 2.1 and lemma 3.5 we get equation 8 and hence the result.

If the above looks abstruse in print, it sounds meaningless in audio. This is a serious drawback when listening to mathematical books on cassette, where it is practically impossible to locate the cross-reference. AsTeR is more effective, since these cross-reference links can be traversed, but traversing each link while listening to a complex proof can be distracting.

Typically, we only glance back at cross-references to get sufficient information to recognize theorem 2.1. AsTeR provides a convenient mechanism for building in such information into the renderings. When rendering a cross-referenceable object such as an equation, AsTeR verbalizes an automatically generated label (e.g., the equation number) and then generates an audible prompt. By pressing a key at this prompt, a more meaningful label can be specified, which will be used in preference to the system-generated label when rendering cross-references.

To continue the current example, when listening to theorem 2.1, suppose the user specifies the label "Fermat's theorem". Then the proof shown earlier would be spoken as:

> By Fermat's theorem and lemma 3.5 we get equation 8 and hence the result.

Of course, the user could have specified labels for the other cross-referenced objects as well, in which case the rendering produced almost obviates the need to look back at the cross-references.

Locating Portions of Interest

Printed books allow the reader to skim the text and quickly locate portions of interest. Experienced readers use several different techniques to achieve this. One of these is to locate an equation or table and then read the text surrounding it. ASTER provides this functionality to some extent.

We explained in Sec. 1.5 that different rules can be activated to change the type of renderings produced. Using this mechanism, we can activate a rendering rule (see Fig. 4.1) that speaks only the equations of a document. When a specific equation is located, rendering can be interrupted and a different rule activated. Using the browser, the listener can now move the current selection to the enclosing hierarchical unit (e.g., the containing paragraph or section) and listen to the surrounding text.

Getting an Overview of a Document

Rendering rules can be activated to obtain different views of a document. For instance, activating rendering rule *quiet* for an object is a convenient way of temporarily skipping over all occurrences of that object —activating *quiet* for object *paragraph* provides a thumb-nail view of a document by skipping all content. This is similar to skipping complex material when first reading a printed document.

We may skip instances of some objects entirely, e.g., source code; in other cases, we may merely defer the reading. This notion of delaying the rendering of an object is aptly captured by the concept of *floating* an object to the end of the enclosing unit. Typesetting systems like (LA)TEX permit the author to float all figures and tables to the end of the containing section or chapter. However, only specific objects can be floated, and this is exclusively under the control of the author, not the reader of the document.

ASTER provides a much more general framework for floating objects. Any object can be floated to the end of any enclosing hierarchical unit —instances of object *footnote* can be floated to the end of the containing paragraph. The ability to float objects is useful when producing audio renderings, since audio takes time, and delaying the rendering of some objects provides an overview.

Rendering using Variable Substitution

When reading complex mathematics in print, we first get a high-level view of an equation and then study its various subexpressions. For example, when presented with a complex equation, an experienced reader of mathematics might view it as an equation with a double summation on the left-hand side and a double integral on the right-hand side, and only then attempt to read the equation in full detail. In a linear audio rendering, the temporal nature of audio prevents a listener from getting such a high-level view. We compensate by providing a variable-substitution rendering style. When it is active, AsTeR replaces sub-expressions in complex mathematics with meaningful phrases. Having thus provided a top-level view, AsTeR then renders these sub-expressions.

Bookmarks

The browser provides a simple bookmark facility for marking positions of interest to be returned to later. Browser command *mark-read-pointer* prompts for a bookmark name and marks the current selection. Later, the listener can move to the object at this marked position by executing browser command *follow-bookmark* with the appropriate bookmark name.

Interfacing AsTeR with other Information Sources

AsTeR has been presented as a system for rendering documents in audio. More generally, AsTeR is a system for speaking structured information. This fact is amply demonstrated by the following example, where we interface AsTeR to the *Emacs* calculator.

The *Emacs* calculator, a public domain symbolic algebra system, provides an excellent source of examples for trying out the variable-substitution rendering style. Creating such an audio interface could be challenging, since the expressions produced are quite complex. However, the flexible design of AsTeR and the power of *Emacs* makes this interface easy. A collection of *Emacs Lisp* functions encodes the calculator output in LaTeX and places it in an *Emacs* buffer, which AsTeR then renders.

A user of the *Emacs* calculator can execute command *read-previous-calc-answer* to have the output rendered by AsTeR. The expression can be browsed, summarized, transformed by applying variable substitution, and rendered in any of the ways described in the context of documents.

2. Recognizing High-Level Document Structure

This chapter describes high-level models for document structure and the extraction of such structure from electronic markup. Our recognizer, a recursive descent parser written in *Lisp*, handles documents encoded in the (LA)TEX family of markup languages: TEX, LATEX and AMS-TEX.

We present the recognizer as follows. Sec. 2.1 describes the high-level models used to capture general document content. Sec. 2.2 presents the models used to capture written mathematics. Sec. 2.3 gives a brief overview of the techniques used to extract structure from documents conforming to our model. (LA)TEX allows the author of a document to extend the markup language by introducing user-defined macros. These are modeled as introducing new object types into the logical structure. Using this model, we describe a flexible method for extending the recognizer to handle (LA)TEX macros in Sec. 2.4. Sec. 2.5 formulates a few guidelines for unambiguous document encodings based on our experience in extracting structure from current-day markup documents. App. A.2 documents the external interface to the recognizer.

2.1 Document Models

All information has high-level structure, and any physical rendering of a document is a projection of this structure onto a particular medium, e.g., printed paper. This high-level structure is itself independent of any particular mode of displaying the information. We have developed high-level models to represent document structure as a first step in audio rendering such structured information. The amount of structural information that can be extracted from the electronic source depends entirely on how the logical structure is marked up. In the context of OCR-based document recognition, this is a function of the quality of the visual rendering being recognized. In the case of both markup-based and OCR-based document recognition, the type of structure that can be extracted varies widely.

Intuitively, there is a hierarchy of document types ordered by the amount of structural information captured, and the ease with which such structure can be recognized. The amount of structural information varies from plain paragraphs and sentences marked up with normal punctuation, all the way up to highly technical documents with footnotes, equations and references. The ease with which the structure can be extracted ranges from the bitmap on a low-resolution fax, through to a postscript file, on upward to a highly marked up SGML file. Given a document instance, the amount of markup information determines which of these logical structures we can extract. Given a plain ASCII document, structural information has to be inferred from the layout of the text, e.g., spacing, vertical alignment and centering. In the case of encodings in markup languages like (LA)TEX, much of the logical structure is explicitly present in the markup. Structure based document encoding systems like SGML provide the potential for extracting the richest possible logical structure, since they separate the layout process from the encoding of the document structure.

Our recognizer captures logical structure present in electronic documents encoded in the TEX family of languages. An important feature of this recognizer is that it works on the entire gamut of encodings, ranging from plain ASCII documents, i.e., no markup, up to documents containing completely unambiguous encodings of the logical structure. Recognition of document structure is an important step in producing audio renderings, since the quality of such renderings is directly determined by the richness of the available structural information.

Our basic document model is the attributed tree. Each hierarchical level of the document is modeled as a node in this tree. Each node can have content, children and attributes. In this respect, our document model is no different from the ones used by SGML[1]. We now introduce the hierarchy of objects used to model documents belonging to the *article* style of LATEX. Since our recognizer is implemented in *CLOS*, an object-oriented language, we will use object-oriented terminology throughout this chapter. Thus, the term *object* typically refers to a *CLOS* object. Further, the terms subclass and subtype are used synonymously.

Class Article

An object of class *article* has *attributes* such as `title`, `author`, `abstract` and `date`. The *children* of object article represent hierarchical structure, e.g., sectional units. The *prologue* of an article is its initial body, i.e., any text occurring before the first sectional unit. Though it would be cleaner to model such initial text as the first child, it is more convenient to handle it as an attribute. This is because (LA)TEX does not specify a complete document type definition (DTD) for articles. This lack of a fully specified DTD results in many of the objects not being well-defined. All objects that capture document content have the same basic model as described above for articles. Note also

[1] The sense in which we use the terms *content* and *attributes* does not always conform to the SGML notion of attributes. *Children* are analogous to the nested element types of SGML.

that LaTeX provides separate *book* and *report* styles. These styles differ from the article style mostly in the kind of layout achieved. The only structural difference is that books and reports in LaTeX can have chapters, while articles cannot. Chapters, sections and subsections are all structures that capture hierarchical document content and are modeled as *sectional units.* The article class of documents defined here therefore encompasses books and reports.

The leaves in the tree structure for documents represent actual content. Plain text is represented as a list of *word* objects, and inline mathematics is represented by object *inline math.* Each node in the document model is linked to its parent and siblings, enabling sophisticated browsing. These links are provided by the *document* base class.

Thus, class *document* provides the following slots:

- **Parent:** Points to parent.
- **Next:** Next sibling.
- **Previous:** Previous sibling.

The following is a brief overview of some of the document objects in our model. All of the following objects inherit from base class *document.*

- **Sectional-unit:**
  - **Attributes:** Title, section number, sectional unit name, e.g., section, subsection.
  - **Children:** List of subsectional units.
  - **Prologue:** List of document objects containing text before first sectional unit.
- **Paragraph:**
  - **Attributes:** None[2].
  - **Children:** None.
  - **Contents:** The paragraph contents as a list of document objects.
- **Word:**
  - **Attributes:** Footnote markers, if any.
  - **Children:** None.
  - **Contents:** String that is the word.
- **Centered paragraph:** subtype of paragraph.
- **Lists:**
  - **Attributes:** None. Enumerated and bulletted lists are subtypes.
  - **Children:** A list of *items.*
  - **Contents:** None.
- **Item:**
  - **Attributes:** Item number, type of bullet, etc.
  - **Children:** None.
  - **Contents:** Contents of the item as a list of document objects.

[2] Though we could model centering etc. as attributes, this is inconsistent with the LaTeX model where such attributed paragraphs are more conveniently treated as new object types.

- **Tables:**
  - **Attributes:** Footnote markers, captions, etc.
  - **Children:** None.
  - **Contents:** The table elements as a doubly linked list.
- **Text block:** A block of text.
  - **Attributes:** Font information, e.g., emphasized text.
  - **Children:** None.
  - **Contents:** A list of document objects.
- **Math equation:** A numbered mathematical equation.
  - **Attributes:** Equation number, cross reference tags, etc.
  - **Content:** A *math object* —see Sec. 2.2.
  - **Children:** None.
- **Math:** Captures both displayed and inline math.
  - **Attribute:** Footnote markers, if any.
  - **Content:** A *math object* representing content.
  - **Children:** None.

Extending Document Logical Structure

LaTeX allows the basic model described above to be extended in two ways:

- By introducing user-defined macros.
- By introducing user-defined environments.

User-defined macros and environments add new object types to the model described above. This will be covered in detail in Sec. 2.4. Suffice it to say for the present that these new objects will extend the basic model outlined above.

The document model is an attributed tree. Cross references are represented by object *cross reference* that contains a pointer to the object being cross-referenced, and this link can be used to traverse the model. The label of a cross-referenceable object is represented as an attribute of that object.

2.2 Representing Mathematical Content

We have designed an internal representation, called the *quasi-prefix* form, for handling mathematical content. It captures the full prefix form of mathematical expressions with operators and simple variables. The tree corresponding to $x+y$ has root $+$ and children x and y and is represented as such internally.

In addition to linearizing the underlying tree structure, mathematical notation uses *visual attributes* such as superscripts and subscripts. We extend the prefix form to capture such visual attributes —hence the name *quasi*-prefix.

The key feature of the quasi-prefix form is that it delays the assignment of semantic interpretation to instances of ambiguous written mathematics.

For example, the superscripts in an expression are represented not as exponents but as attribute *superscript.* This is because the meaning of these visual attributes is context dependent. Assigning one of the several possible interpretations at the recognition step is unduly restrictive in a fully flexible rendering system. For example, interpreting the superscript as an exponent would result in x^2 being recognized correctly, but A^T being incorrectly recognized. Further, it would be impossible to later distinguish between the correct and incorrect interpretations. The quasi-prefix form captures the mathematical notation itself, leaving the assignment of semantic interpretation to a later step. By doing so, we can represent content where we do not have sufficient semantic information. Thus, $D_x^1 u$ might denote the first derivative of u with respect to x in a specific context. The superscript and subscript might mean something entirely different in another context, e.g., as in $D_n a_n$. If more contextual information is available at the rendering step, ASTER can speak A^T as "cap a transpose". In the absence of such contextual information, the system can still produce an audio notation that maps different features of the written notation to unique audio dimensions.

At the same time, the quasi-prefix form is sufficiently rich to permit renderings that are independent of the order in which the written symbols appear on paper. Linear renderings with the rendering-order hard-coded into the system can be produced with a simpler representation, e.g., a linear list, or even the TEX encoding itself. This was shown by TEXTALK, a string-substitution based program that directly transformed TEX source to produce linear renderings [Ram91, Ram92].

As an example, assume that `\kronecker`[3] is defined as an infix binary operator. Given the expression $a \otimes b$ encoded as `$a\kronecker b$`, we can write a rendering rule for object *kronecker* represented in the quasi-prefix form to produce "a kronecker product b". This rendering can be produced by TEXTALK as well, but a simpler list-like representation restricts the system to this one form of rendering. Using the quasi-prefix form, ASTER can also produce "the kronecker product of a and b".

Thus, even though the quasi-prefix form captures only the information present in the TEX encoding, it is still flexible enough to permit more sophisticated processing.

This power is necessary in overcoming the passive nature of listening. In producing printed output, it is sufficient to produce one view; once the information has been presented visually, a person reading the material can access it in any desired order. TEX itself therefore never builds up an internal representation like the quasi-prefix form; its purpose is to typeset the input according to a fixed set of rules, and the TEX encoding directly reflects the linear order[4] in which expressions appear on paper. Thus, here, the displayed

[3] TEX does not provide this operator, and it will have to be defined as a macro. We describe how ASTER is extended to handle such macros in Sec. 2.4.

[4] TEX does not itself impose this; one can always write a macro\reverse that displays its arguments in reverse order.

information is passive while the person reading it is active. The situation in presenting information orally is exactly the opposite; the information flows past a passive listener. In order to achieve effective oral communication, it is therefore important to be able to present multiple views of the information.

Math Object Encapsulates Quasi-Prefix Form

To represent the quasi-prefix form, we extend the attributed tree model defined in the previous section with object *math object.* We define six such attributes in Fig. 2.1. A math object may have any or all of these attributes.

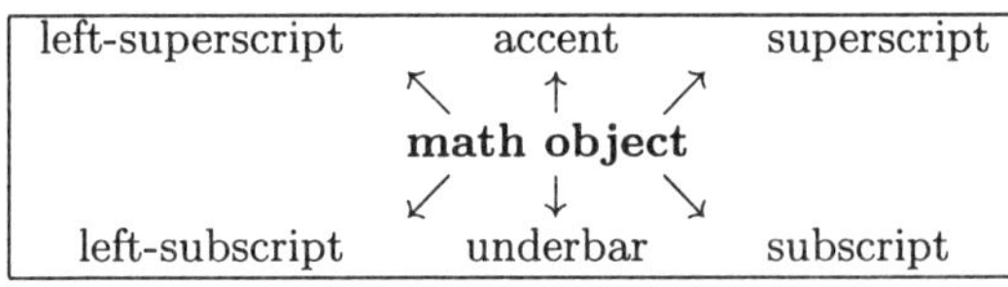

Fig. 2.1. A math object with attributes. Each of the attributes themselves contain math objects.

An attribute can have a math object as content.

Here are the basic object types in this representation:

- **Math object:** Basic representation for mathematical content. It is a subtype of *document.*
  - **Attributes:** A list of *math attribute* objects.
  - **Content:** String representing the content.
  - **Children:** List of children. Each child is a math object.
- **Math attribute:** Captures visual annotations. *Superscript*, *subscript*, etc. have the same structure and are subclasses of class *math attribute.*
  - **Name:** Attribute name, e.g., superscript, accent.
  - **Content:** Contents of this attribute as a math object.

The structure is recursive. For example, x_1^k is represented by the math object

- **Content:** "x".
- **Children:** None.
- **Attributes:** A list of attribute objects:
  - **Superscript:** Subtype of *math attribute.*
    - **Name:** Superscript.
    - **Content:** "k".
  - **Subscript:** subtype of object *math attribute.*
    - **Name:** Subscript.
    - **Content:** "1".

The representation can capture mathematical expressions with arbitrarily complex visual attributes. Let M denote the math object shown above. Then

$$x^{x_1^k}_{x_1^k}$$

would be represented by math object M' shown below:

- **Content:** "x".
- **Superscript:** M.
- **Subscript:** M.

Refining the Quasi-Prefix Form

In Sec. 2.1, we mentioned that all objects in our document model are linked. This is true of the objects appearing in the quasi-prefix representation. Each node in the tree is linked to its parent, as well as to its previous and next siblings. Math attributes have their parent link set to the object being attributed.

We refine the quasi-prefix form by adding the following subtypes. This makes recognizing and handling complex mathematical content cleaner.

We first introduce object *math subformula*, which is used to capture subexpressions appearing within the { and } of (LA)TEX. Object *math subformula* can be thought of as being the math equivalent of object *text block* described in Sec. 2.1. It has the following structure:

- **Attribute:** Visual attributes.
- **Content:** The mathematical content represented as a *math object*.

Object *math subformula* can be intuitively thought of as a dummy object that encapsulates an expression.

We need object *math subformula* to represent expressions of the form:

$$\overbrace{x+\cdots+x}^{k \text{ times}}$$

$$\underbrace{x+y+z}_{>0}$$

In representing each of the above examples, object *math subformula* is essential in capturing the expression to which the overbrace/underbrace applies.

To enable recognition of written mathematics, tokens have to be appropriately classified. Our classification of tokens when processing written mathematics is inspired by appendix F of the TEX Book, [Knu84].

> The symbols divide naturally into groups based on their mathematical class (Ord, Op, Bin, Rel, Open, Close, or Punct), ...

We introduce subtypes of object *math object* to correspond to each token type:

- **Ordinary:** TeX ord. Letters, numbers and some miscellaneous symbols.
- **Big operator:** TeX Op. The *large* operators that typically appear as unary operators, e.g., $\int$, $\sum$, $\bigcup$.
- **Binary operator:** TeX Bin. The binary operators, e.g., $+$, $\cup$.
- **Relational operator:** TeX Rel, e.g., $<$, $\geq$. We subdivide the TeX Rel class into relational and arrow operators.
- **Arrow operators:** Arrows such as $\nearrow$, $\leftharpoonup$.
- **Mathematical function:** Plain TeX and LaTeX define sin etc. as macros. We introduce an object type, *mathematical function* to represent these.
- **Open delimiter:** TeX Open, e.g., (, {.
- **Close delimiter:** TeX Close, e.g.,), }.
- **Math punctuation :** TeX Punct —punctuation marks.

Written mathematical notation uses *juxtaposition* as an infix operator. Juxtaposition, as in $a(b + c)$, mostly denotes multiplication, but can mean function application in certain contexts —$f(x + y)$. We introduce a new operator to represent juxtaposition, and to define it precisely, we also assert that all mathematical variables are single letters. Thus, *cab* is represented as the juxtaposition of three *ordinary* objects. This assertion is not specific to our internal representation, rather, it specifies the concrete syntax used in the electronic markup and reflects the choice made in the design of TeX. We do allow mathematical variables made up of more than one character, but these should be clearly marked up as such, e.g., as $\mbox{cab} = cab$, by using `\mbox` as in `$\mbox{cab}=cab$`.

The classification of a math object is defined using the following command:

(*define-math-classification <token> <classification>*)

In certain special cases, the predefined classification shown above can be modified. A good example of this is recognizing a mathematical text that consistently uses the letters f, g and h to denote functions. Using the predefined classification, the recognizer would treat f as object *ordinary*, leading to $f(x)$ being represented as the juxtaposition of two objects, namely, f and (x). Declaring f to be a mathematical function by executing

(*define-math-classification* f *mathematical-function-name*)

results in occurrences of f being treated as a function. Hence, $f(x)$ is correctly recognized as a function application. Note that the correct interpretation of such notation is more important for browsing than for speaking the expression.

2.3 Constructing High-Level Representations

This section describes the techniques used to extract high-level models from the (LA)TeX source. A recursive descent parsing algorithm is used to construct the tree structure for document content conforming to the model described in Sec. 2.1. This algorithm is modified to construct the quasi-prefix form. These refinements enable our recognizer to correctly handle ambiguous mathematical notation, as in the expression $\sin 2x = 2 \sin x \cos x$. We use a modified version of the conventional operator-precedence approach for constructing the quasi-prefix form. With the refinements and heuristics outlined in this section, our algorithm successfully recognizes written mathematical notation from a wide variety of sources.

2.3.1 Lexical Analysis and Recognition

Lisp-CLOS was chosen to implement AsTeRbecause of its powerful development environment and object-oriented features. However, *Lisp-CLOS* lacks tools such as lexical analyzers and parser generators, e.g., *LEX* and *YACC*. As a convenient way of getting the best of both worlds, we designed a lexical analyzer called *lispify* in *LEX* that outputs the input (LA)TeX source in a canonical list representation. This list is then read in by a recursive descent parser written in *Lisp*. The general form of this list is (*token* <*body*>), where <*token*> identifies the type of content encapsulated by the list and <*body*> represents the content. The recognizer returns a *document* object that encapsulates the document instance being recognized. For example, given the (LA)TeX input

```
\begin{center}
This is a sample document.
\end{center}
```

LISPIFY produces

```
(center "This"  "is"  "a"  "sample"  "document" ".")
```

LISPIFY handles all of (LA)TeX concrete syntax.

The recursive descent parser examines the *token* at the front of the input list and calls a token-specific processing function on the rest of the list. Thus, given the input (*token* <*body*>), the recognizer executes

(funcall (get-parser *token*) <*body*>)

The technique described so far is sufficient for handling sections, enumerated lists and other textual content.

2.3.2 Constructing the Quasi-Prefix Form

The recognizer processes the mathematical content to construct the quasi-prefix form described in Sec. 2.2. For example, given the input `$a+b$`, *LISPIFY* produces

```
(inline-math  "a"  "+"  "b" )
```

Converting a list as shown above to prefix form is a simple exercise and can be found in most programming language texts. Our implementation is based on the infix to prefix converter in the text on Common Lisp by Winston and Horn[5] [HW89].

Function *inf-to-pre* performs the infix-to-prefix conversion. The input to this function is a list of math objects that have been processed using the classification given in Sec. 2.2. Each element of this list is a math object with content and attributes but no children. Note that the contents of the attributes are first converted to quasi-prefix form. For example, when recognizing $x_{k-1} + x_k + x_{k+1}$, the input is first converted to a list of five math objects containing the quasi-prefix representation for x_{k-1}, $+$, x_k, $+$ and x_{k+1} respectively. This is achieved by collecting the attributes that appear on each math object and processing their content recursively. Converting such a list to prefix form is now no different than processing $a + b$.

We now extend this algorithm to handle ambiguous mathematical notation. Conventional parsing techniques fail, since written mathematics does not adhere to a rigorous set of precedence rules. For example, the expression $\sin 2n\pi$ means $\sin(2n\pi)$ rather than $\sin(2) * n\pi$, even though function application is normally assigned the highest precedence. Moreover, $\sin a \cos b$ means $\sin a * \cos b$ rather than $\sin(a \cos b)$. We have taken many such anomalies into account.

The precedence table for operators Table 2.1 lists operators in ascending order of precedence. Only one operator is shown at each level.

Functions *define-precedence* and *remove-precedence* allow the user to modify the precedence table. These, however, are not for use by a casual user of AsTeR, since changes to the precedence table without a clear understanding of the recognition algorithm can cause unexpected behavior.

As pointed out earlier, precedence rules alone are not sufficient to handle written mathematics. We adapt the algorithm by using the following heuristics:

- The big operators, e.g., $\int$ and $\sum$, are treated as unary. Everything up to the next operator of lower precedence than the operator in question is considered part of the operand of the big operator. Thus, in the expression

[5] We would like to thank the authors for providing electronic access to the LaTeX source for their book. It proved an invaluable online Lisp reference while implementing AsTeR.

Table 2.1. Precedence table for mathematical operators.

Level	Description	Examples
0	tex-infix-operator	$\frac{a}{b}$
1	math-list-operator	a, b
2	conditional-operator	$a : b$
3	quantifier	$\forall a$
4	relational-operator	$a = b$
5	arrow-operator	$a \longrightarrow b$
6	big-operator	$\sum_a b$
7	logical-or	$a \vee b$
8	logical-and	$a \wedge b$
9	addition	$a + b$
10	multiplication	$a * b$
11	mathematical-function	$\sin a$
12	juxtaposition	ab
13	unary-minus	$\neg a$

$$\sum_{\substack{1\le i\le p\\1\le j\le q\\1\le k\le r}} a_{ij}b_{jk}c_{ki} = 1$$

everything up to the = sign is treated as the summand. This technique is particularly useful in recognizing expressions like $x + \sum_i a_i = 0$. By our heuristic, the summation is correctly recognized as the second argument to the + sign. Further, the summand is terminated by the = sign. The expression is now equivalent to recognizing $a+c = 0$, which can be handled by the standard algorithm.

- The integral operator can have an optional delimiter, as in $\int_1^\infty f\,dx$. If the dx is present and is recognizable i.e., has been marked up as `\d{x}` as opposed to `dx`, it is recognized as the closing delimiter; the variable of integration[6] is inferred. However, this closing delimiter may not always be available —it may be encoded ambiguously, as in `$\int f dx$`, or the integral itself may not require a closing dx, as in $\int f$. In the former case, our recognizer treats the juxtaposition fdx as the integrand. Though this may seem incorrect, it is in fact exactly what the typeset output means. In the latter case, the earlier rule (treating the operand of a big operator to be everything up to the first operator of lower precedence) applies. Hence, we can correctly recognize $x + \int f = 0$.
- The closing delimiter dx is treated as such only if it occurs at the top level. Thus, in `$\frac{\dx}{x}$`, the `\dx` does not end the integrand. This allows us to recognize such integrals correctly, but we cannot now infer the variable of integration. There seems to be no clean solution for this problem. Written mathematical notation relies on the fact that dx means $1 \cdot dx$ and the integrand is therefore $\frac{1}{x}$.

[6] We have also built in the macros `\dx`, `\dy`, ... as special cases.

- Function application is treated as right associative. This results in $\sin a \cos b$ being interpreted correctly. Since juxtaposition has been assigned a higher precedence than function application, $\sin a \cos b$ continues to be recognized correctly. The following equation is a good example of such ambiguous notation —note the complete absence of parentheses:

$$2 \sin 2n\pi \cos 2n\pi = \sin 4n\pi$$

- In written mathematics, delimiters do not always match. For example, $(0, 1]$ denotes a semi-open interval. There are also cases where there is no matching closing delimiter. The recognizer is aware of such anomalies and handles them correctly. When it sees an open delimiter, it scans forward to the end of the math expression for the first matching close delimiter of the same kind. If one is found, then all of the input up to this point is treated as the delimited expression. If no matching close delimiter of the same kind is found, then the first unmatched close delimiter delimits the input. Otherwise, the occurrence is treated as an unmatched delimiter.
- The ! is one of the few postfix operators used in written mathematics. This is treated as a special case, and we confirm that the ! is indeed a factorial sign by making sure that it does not have any attributes. Thus, $!_k$ is not a factorial symbol.

2.4 Macros Introduce New Object Types

The previous sections described our document model and the techniques used to construct high-level representations given documents that conform to this model. The TEX macro facility [Knu84, Knu86] allows the definition of new markup commands, making (LA)TEX extensible. Macros permit the author to abstract away layout details when writing the document. To give an example, the command `\kronecker` is not present in (LA)TEX. An author can extend (LA)TEX by defining

```
\newcommand{\kronecker}{\raisebox{1pt}{\:\otimes\:}}
```

and then write

```
$ A \kronecker B$
```

The new definition for `\kronecker` has extended the markup language. LATEX [Lam86] itself is a good example of how TEX macros can be used to implement a language for encoding document structure.

The presence of user-defined macros in documents presents an interesting challenge for a system like ASTER. Our goal is to handle books and technical documents written in (LA)TEX, so recognizing the extended logical structure introduced by the definition of new macros is therefore essential. In general, macro expansion can perform any arbitrary computation permitted by the

TeX language. Hence, it is impossible to directly translate the macro expansion into an audio rendering. The TeX primitives are visual layout operators, and translating a TeX macro directly into an audio rendering rule would imply a one-to-one mapping between the visual and audio rendering.

As explained in Sec. 1.1, visual renderings are attuned to a two-dimensional display, and audio renderings need to be attuned to the features of an auditory display. Further, expanding a TeX macro loses structural information; when all macros in a document have been expanded, only the visual layout remains.

The first step in solving this problem is to represent user-defined macros in our high-level document model. Producing audio renderings of such instances will then be equivalent to rendering any other object present in the model.

Macro definitions introduce new object types. Thus, defining `\kronecker` is equivalent to adding object *kronecker* to the set of objects present in the document model. A macro definition in (LA)TeX has two parts; the first part declares the macro and its number of arguments; the second part specifies how instances of this macro call are to be displayed. Translating this to the object-oriented model, the first part of the macro introduces a new object type; the second part is a rendering rule for instances of this object.

We first describe how the recognizer is extended to handle instances of the new object introduced by a macro definition. We specify the following information about the new macro and the associated object type:

Macro name: The name of the macro.

Number of arguments: The number of arguments taken by this macro.

Processing function: Name of a processing function that parses instances of this macro call. This function is synthesized automatically.

Object name: Name of the new object type introduced by this macro. Calls to this macro appearing in the document will be converted to instances of this object type.

Precedence: If the new object is an operator, its precedence is declared in terms of one of the existing operators. See Table 2.1 for the precedence table.

Super classes: Super classes of this new object. The new object will inherit the behavior of its super classes. Thus, since `\kronecker` will be used as a binary operator, we can declare it as such.

Arguments are called: Contextual names for the arguments of this macro. For example, the left-hand side of an inference is called its *premise*, the right-hand side its *conclusion*. If `\inference` is defined as a macro with two arguments, then we can supply these contextual names to *define-text-object*. Such information is used to generate sophisticated audio renderings.

This information is supplied by calling *Lisp* macro *define-text-object*. We illustrate this in the case of `\kronecker` in Fig. 2.2. The *Lisp* macro itself will be described in Sec. 2.4.1.

```
(define-text-object :macro-name "kronecker" :number-args 0
  :processing-function kronecker-expand
  :object-name kronecker
  :supers (binary-operator) :precedence  multiplication)
```

Fig. 2.2. Extending the recognizer to handle user-defined macros.

Note that our recognizer has more information about the new macro than TeX. This is consistent with the fact that our internal representation is richer than the TeX representation, as described in Sec. 2.2.

To summarize, we model a macro as:

- Introducing a new object type, thereby extending the logical structure.
- Specifying how to display objects of this type.

A call to the macro in the document creates an object of the type introduced by that macro.

To continue with the example of `kronecker`, given

```
$A \kronecker B$
```

LISPIFY converts it to

```
(inline-math  "A"  (cs   "kronecker" ) "B" )
```

LISPIFY marks the (LA)TeX macro instance as a a control sequence (*cs*). The recursive descent recognizer performs the following steps on encountering calls to macro `\kronecker`:

- Retrieve the appropriate processing function for this control sequence. In this case it is the automatically synthesized function *kronecker-expand.*
- Call this function with as many tokens from the input as is required by the TeX macro. In this case, this is 0, since macro `\kronecker` takes no arguments.

Function *kronecker-expand* constructs an instance of object *kronecker.* At this point, this instance of object *kronecker* has its *children* set to *null.* The input list is thus converted to a list containing three *math objects* shown below.

$$(\textit{ordinary kronecker ordinary})$$

In the above list, only the types of the objects are shown. This list is now processed by function *inf-to-pre* to produce the quasi-prefix form. Since class *kronecker* is a subclass of *binary-operator* with the same precedence as multiplication, the result is a tree with *kronecker* as the root and with two children, one each corresponding to A and B.

In the above, A and B may be arbitrarily complex pieces of (LA)TeX markup; the recursive nature of the recognition algorithm will set the children of object *kronecker* to the operands in their processed form. For example, we can now build an internal representation for the following equation:

$$(A \otimes B)^T = A^T \otimes B^T$$

which would be written in (LA)TEX as

```
\[ (A \kronecker B)^{T} = A^{T} \kronecker B^{T}  \]
```

2.4.1 How *define-text-object* Works

Lisp macro *define-text-object* is quite involved. In this overview, we use the call shown in Fig. 2.2 to illustrate the various steps. A call to macro *define-text-object* performs the following steps:

Define class: Generate the class definition for the new object type. In our example, it produces:

```
(defclass kronecker (binary-operator)
  ((contents :initform nil :initarg :contents
             :accessor contents))
  (:documentation "class kronecker
   corresponding to  document macro kronecker"))
```

If the corresponding macro takes n arguments, i.e., number-args $= n$ in Fig. 2.2, then the new object type is defined to have a slot *arguments*. This slot will hold a list containing the result of processing the n arguments of the (LA)TEX macro call.

Define processing function: Define a processing function that is called to process instances of the (LA)TEX macro call. The function applies the recursive-descent algorithm to the next `number-args` tokens from the input stream. In the current example, the function generated is:

```
(defun kronecker-expand (&rest arguments)
  "automatically generated processing function"
  (assert (= (length arguments) 0)
          nil "wrong number of arguments")
  (let* ((self (make-instance 'kronecker))
         (processor (if (math-p self)
                        #'process-argument-as-math
                        #'process-argument-as-text)))
    (unless (= number-args  0)
      (setf (arguments self)
            (loop for arg in arguments collect
                  (funcall processor arg)))) self))
```

where variable `number-args` is bound to the value of the `number-args` keyword argument in the lexical scope in which the function definition is evaluated. Functions *process-argument-as-math* and *process-argument-as-text* apply the recursive descent parser to their argument; the former parses mathematical content, the latter processes plain text.

Define accessor methods: If `number-args` $\neq 0$, accessor method *argument* is generated. Method *argument* takes two arguments, an instance o of the new object and an integer n, and retrieves the result of processing argument n of the corresponding call to the (LA)TEX macro. It is used in the rendering rules to retrieve different pieces of a (LA)TEX macro call. See Sec. 2.4.2 for an example of its use. Assuming that `number-args` $= n$, this method looks like:

```
(defmethod argument ((n integer) (kronecker kronecker))
  "automatically generated argument accessor"
  (assert (<= n (length (arguments kronecker ))) nil
   "not that many arguments.")
  (elt (arguments kronecker) (- n 1)))
```

We take advantage of the generic dispatch provided by *CLOS* and define an instance of the above method with its arguments reversed —this avoids having to remember the order of arguments to function *argument* when writing rendering rules.

Define precedence: If the `precedence` keyword argument is supplied, an appropriate call to *define-precedence* is generated:

```
(define-precedence  "kronecker" :same-as 'multiplication)
```

Install macro definition: Finally, the (LA)TEX macro is installed in a global table that records all known (LA)TEX macros.

```
(define-tex-macro "kronecker" 0 'kronecker-expand)
```

This specifies that the macro being defined takes 0 arguments and calls to it should be processed using function *kronecker-expand.*

The call to the *Lisp* macro *define-text-object* shown in this example produces 123 lines of *Lisp* code.

2.4.2 Rendering Instances of User-Defined Macros

Our system of rendering rules will be described in detail in Chap. 4. Such rules are written in AFL, our language for audio formatting, described in Chap. 3. Here, we show a small example of such a rendering rule for a user-defined macro. In the following, we use *CLOS* generic function *read-aloud,* described in Chap. 4. For the present, let us assume that function *read-aloud* executes the necessary actions to render its argument. After executing the appropriate call to *define-text-object* for the (LA)TEX macro `\inference`, which is defined as

```
\newcommand\inference[2]{\frac{#1}{#2}}
```

to render instances of calls to `\inference`, we can define

```
(defmethod read-aloud((inference inference))
  "Sample read-aloud method for object inference.
Demonstrates how macro arguments are accessed when rendering. "
  (read-aloud (argument 1 inference))
  (read-aloud "implies")
  (read-aloud (argument 2 inference)))
```

If we wished to produce a rendering that inverts the order in which the arguments to macro `\inference` are rendered, we would define:

```
(defmethod read-aloud((inference inference))
  "Renders inference with arguments reversed."
  (read-aloud "We know that ")
  (read-aloud (argument 2 inference))
  (read-aloud "because")
  (read-aloud (argument 1 inference)))
```

A flexible method for switching among different rendering rules to obtain different "audio views" of the same object is described in Sec. 4.1.

Defining New Environments in LaTeX

As outlined in Sec. 2.1, the document model in LaTeX can be extended by defining new environments. Typically, a new environment is defined to achieve specific kinds of layout, e.g., for typesetting conjectures and lemmas. We treat such environment definitions as adding new objects to the document model. The approach used is very similar to handling user-defined macros, though somewhat simpler. Object *new-environment* is used as a base class for all user-defined environments. The principal difference between objects introduced by user-defined macros and user-defined environments is that *new-environment* objects can be labeled and later cross referenced. The *Lisp* macro *define-new-environment* does the necessary bookkeeping involved in tracking such cross-referenceable objects. These properties are provided by the class definition for object *new-environment*.

2.5 Unambiguous Document Encodings

We formulate a few guidelines for encoding document content unambiguously based on our experience in recognizing structure from electronic markup. A document that adheres to these guidelines makes recognition easier. This is not to say that we cannot handle documents that do not conform to these guidelines, but our recognizer can extract more information from such unambiguous encodings. In general, we feel that electronic encodings conforming to these guidelines will be easier to maintain and enable multiple uses of the electronic source.

(LA)TeX macros provide an excellent solution to the problem of capturing context specific information in the document encoding. The same visual layout may be used to display disparate concepts. Encoding instances of such ambiguous notation by using well-designed macros abstracts out the layout details from the document encoding, and allows a recognizer to identify the different concepts correctly. We illustrate this with a concrete example.

The visual layout of stacking one mathematical object above another, separated by a horizontal line (horizontal rule), could be used in several contexts.

- **Fraction:** $\frac{1+\sqrt{5}}{2}$
- **Inference rule:** $\frac{X=Y, Y=Z}{X=Z}$

Using the encoding `\frac{object-1}{object-2}` in both cases makes it impossible to disambiguate between the various interpretations. When an author wishes to use the same layout to mean different things, the different occurrences should be marked up distinctly. For instance, in LaTeX, the author could extend the markup language by defining two new macros:

1. `\newcommand{\fraction}[2]{\frac{#1}{#2}}`.
2. `\newcommand{\inference}[2]{\frac{#1}{#2}}`.

Visual math notation is inherently ambiguous and derives most of its expressiveness by freely overloading standard visual-layout operators. (LA)TeX allows an author complete flexibility in producing mathematical notation by providing the primitives needed to produce such notation. It would be too restrictive to insist that the complete semantics of a mathematical object appear explicitly in the markup, since this would make inventing new notation cumbersome, if not impossible. So, to an extent, we will never be able to attach semantic meaning to every object in the document. However, we insist that document encodings should not use identical markup to represent objects that have the same visual layout but different meanings. This will allow a recognizer to process the objects in the document according to context and later permit context specific renderings.

In addition, an electronic encoding should not use (LA)TeX layout operators within the body of the document. This principle is in fact well-accepted within the electronic-documents community, but it is not adhered to as often as one would like. Document encodings that violate this requirement will become fewer with widespread use of editors that allow an author to easily encode document structure.

What we are saying is no different than the well-accepted programming standard that stipulates that function names should reflect the computation they perform. A well-designed macro library is like a well-designed subroutine library. To cite a quotation from the TeX Book:

> It is much easier to use macros than to define them. ... The use of macro libraries, in fact, mirrors almost exactly the use of subroutine libraries for programming languages. There are the same levels of specialization, from publicly shared subroutines to special subroutines within a single program, and there is the same need for a programmer with particular skills to define the subroutines.
>
> PETER BROWN, *Macro Processors* (1974)

To summarize, here are some guidelines for unambiguous document encoding:

- Avoid use of layout operators like `\hskip` and `\vskip` in (LA)TeX.

– Use different macros to encode semantically distinct objects that have the same visual layout.

Electronic encodings have not always followed these rules, since the markup was viewed purely as a means of producing the visual rendering. Our work points out that the same encoding can be put to multiple uses; it is therefore important to apply principles of good software design to produce well structured document encodings.

3. AFL: Audio Formatting Language

In Chap. 2, we described the internal representations used to capture document structure and content. This internal representation is rendered in audio by applying audio rendering rules written in AFL, a language for audio formatting.

AFL can be viewed as the audio analogue of visual formatting languages like Postscript. Postscript provides primitives to write visual rendering rules; AFL provides the corresponding audio rendering primitives. A set of rendering rules written in AFL manipulate the *audio formatter*: the logical device that controls the (possibly) multiple components (e.g., speech and sound) of the audio system.

The audio formatter has *state*. The kind of voice used, the speed of speech, the pitch of the voice, the type of sounds generated, etc. are all determined by the current state of the formatter. AFL, a block structured language, captures this state in an AFL program variable, and AFL statements manipulate this state. This chapter describes AFL, which has been implemented as an extension to *Common Lisp*. Thus, the AFL programmer can use all the standard constructs provided by *Lisp*.

Sec. 3.1, gives an overview of AFL and the design issues that have been addressed. Sec. 3.2 presents AFL in its most important setting, as a language capable of controlling a single component —a speech synthesizer. Sec. 3.3 describes how AFL handles an audio formatter with multiple components. Sec. 3.4 describes AFL in the context of non-speech audio, and Sec. 3.5 describes the pronunciation component of our present system. Sec. 3.6 provides some concluding remarks. App. A.3 documents the various AFL statements.

3.1 Overview

An audio formatter (a logical device that produces audio output) can have several components, e.g., a speech component and multiple sound components. The state space of the audio formatter, henceforth referred to as the *audio space*, is modeled as the direct sum (or cross product) of the state spaces of these components. Thus, given an audio formatter with n components, its state is an n-tuple $(s_1, s_2, \cdots, s_n)$, where s_i is the state of component i. Each component subspace is a multi-dimensional space, with dimensions corresponding to parameters that can be modified on the corresponding hardware component. In AsTeR we have:

$$\text{audio-space} = \text{speech-space} \times \text{sound-space} \times \text{pronunciation}.$$

AFL state variables capture the current and global states of each component space. The AFL block introduces a new lexical scope with local copies of all the current component-state variables. For example, variable **current-speech-state** is the local state of the speech component (in the current block) and **global-speech-state** is its global state. Each component subspace provides operators for moving in that subspace. Operators select points (either by name or by applying transformations to other points) and are used to form AFL expressions. When a block terminates (prematurely or otherwise), effects of all local assignments made within that block are undone. Components of the audio formatter may have independent threads of control. AFL provides primitives for synchronizing these multiple threads. Blocks also serve as implicit *cobegin* statements; events started within a block are completed before the block terminates.

AFL rendering rules typically introduce a new block, set the state of the audio formatter and execute some actions. When the audio rendering has been completed, the block terminates, resulting in the state of the audio formatter being reset.

Here is an outline of a typical AFL rendering rule:

```
(def-reading-rule ...
    (afl:new-block ... (afl:local-set-state ...) ...))
```

3.2 The Speech Component

We present AFL in the simple context of an audio formatter having a single component —a speech synthesizer. The principal purpose of the speech component is to produce speech —it provides statement

(*afl:send-text* <*text*>).

This statement sends <*text*> to the speech device. In addition, the speech component provides primitives for producing the right intonational structure. The speech generation statements are summarized in Table 3.2.

The speaking voice can be varied with respect to several speech synthesis parameters. We define the *speech space* as a multi-dimensional space, where each dimension corresponds to a synthesizer parameter. At any given time, the *speech state*, a point in this space, determines the kind of voice used when speech generation statements are executed. Changing a voice parameter amounts to moving in this space. The abstraction of a speech space imposes structure on the set of discrete states provided by the voice synthesizer. This structure will be used to advantage in producing renderings of nested information structures. The abstraction of a *speech space* also keeps the speech component of AFL hardware independent —synthesizers vary widely in both the kind of parameters provided as well as how these are modified.

In any AFL program segment, global variable **global-speech-state** and local variable **current-speech-state** (modifiable by the program segment) refer to one of these speech states. When a session of interactive rendering is begun, these variables are set to the initial state of the audio formatter.

The AFL Block

The AFL block

(*afl:new-block <statements>*)

introduces a local instance of variable **current-speech-state**. This instance is set to the instance of **current-speech-state** that was referenceable just before execution of the block, and *<statements>* are executed within this new local scope. Within the block, all free occurrences of **current-speech-state** refer to the new local variable. Further, this local variable describes the state of the audio formatter, so changes to it immediately affect the voice synthesizer. Upon termination of the block, local variable **current-speech-state** is destroyed, and the audio formatter is reset to its pre-existing state. The programmer has no control over the name of this local state variable and cannot create other local variables using the AFL block.

Execution of statement *(terminate-block)* causes the currently-executing block to terminate immediately. A browser can execute this statement when the audio rendering of an object is to be terminated prematurely because of an interrupt from the user.

AFL blocks are simpler than the standard block construct provided by full-blown programming languages. For the purpose of audio formatting, where the major task is to control the parameters of the speech space, our experience has shown that the AFL block is more than adequate. Further, our simplified version of the block prevents rendering rules from making changes to the state of the audio formatter that could persist after termination of a block. Such changes, which would be possible with the conventional block, would also complicate the implementation, which has to maintain the connection between the state of local variable **current-speech-state** and the voice synthesizer itself.

Dimensions for the MultiVoice

In the previous subsection, we mentioned that the speech space has several dimensions, which might depend on the particular voice synthesizer being used. In order to make our presentation more concrete, we now describe the dimensions that can be used with the MultiVoice synthesizer.

The MultiVoice provides nine predefined voices, which are modeled as distinguished points (constants) in the speech space. We list below the MultiVoice names for the voices, together with the name used within AFL for them.

Perfect Paul	*'afl:paul*	Huge Harry	*'afl:harry*
Frail Frank	*'afl:frank*	Doctor Dennis	*'afl:dennis*
Beautiful Betty	*'afl:betty*	Rough Rita	*'afl:rita*
Uppity Ursula	*'afl:ursula*	Whispering Wendy	*'afl:wendy*
Kit the Kid	*'afl:kid*		

A user can save a particular speech state in a variable and refer to it later. For example, execution of the statement[1]

(*save-point-in-speech-space <name> *current-speech-state**)

saves the value of **current-speech-state** in program variable *<name>*. Statement

(*get-point-in-speech-space <name>*)

retrieves the value saved in variable *<name>*. Male and female voices are to be thought of as lying in distinct disconnected components of the speech space, since it is not possible to move from a male voice to a female voice simply by changing parameters that affect voice quality[2]. Switching from a male to a female voice is thus analogous to changing fonts, while modifying voice quality parameters is like scaling different features of a specific font.

The MultiVoice parameters (and their default values) that are implemented as dimensions in AFL are shown in Table 3.1. They are: the speech rate, the volumes of the speaker and the earphone port, five voice-quality parameters, and seven parameters that deal with pitch and intonation. The column labeled "step size" will be discussed later on.

We assume that these dimensions are available and can be changed by the statements that are defined in the next subsection.

AFL Statements

We now describe five other AFL statements used to change speech-space variables. In the descriptions, *<point>* denotes any expression that evaluates to a point in the speech space, *<name>* is a variable that may contain a point

[1] Switching to a new voice causes a slight pause in the speech, so it is inadvisable to change the speaking voice in the middle of a sentence, since this ruins the intonation.

[2] This is because female voices use a different noising source.

Table 3.1. Implemented MultiVoice parameters

Dimension	Min	Max	Initial	step size	Units
afl:speech-rate	120	550	180	25	Words/Min
Volume					
afl:left-volume	0	100	50	5	dB
afl:right-volume	0	100	50	5	dB
Voice quality					
afl:breathiness	0	100	0	10	DB
afl:lax-breathiness	0	100	0	25	%
afl:smoothness	0	100	3	20	%
afl:richness	0	100	70	10	%
afl:laryngilization	0	100	0	10	%
Pitch and Intonation					
afl:baseline-fall	0	40	18	10	Hz
afl:hat-rise	2	100	18	10	Hz
afl:stress-rise	1	100	32	20	Hz
afl:assertiveness	0	100	100	25	%
afl:quickness	0	100	0	10	%
afl:average-pitch	50	350	122	10	Hz
afl:pitch-range	0	100	100	10	%

in the speech space, and *<dimension>* is the name of a dimension in speech space.

Statement *initialize-speech-space* must be executed before any operations are performed on speech-space variables. It assigns default initial values to AFL variables **current-speech-state** and **global-speech-state**.

Statements

(local-set-state <point>*)*

and

(global-set-state <point>*)*

assign *<point>* to **current-speech-state** and **global-speech-state** respectively. Assignment statement *local-set-state* synchronizes implicitly with events on the speech component, i.e., execution of the assignment waits until all prior speech events have completed. This synchronization is necessary, since in general the host computer controlling the audio formatter executes instructions much faster than the speech synthesizer.

The two statements given above are conventional assignment statements, but they are only used to change the two AFL state variables.

Languages like TeX and PostScript provide for the application of a global scaling to a rendering. The speech space provides similar functionality. The speech component uses a final filter with the scale factor for each dimension initially set to unity, and execution of

(set-final-scale-factor <dimension> <value>*)*

changes the final scale factor for dimension *<dimension>* to *<value>*. As an example of its use, interrupting an audio rendering and executing

(set-final-scale-factor afl:speech-rate 2)

and then resuming causes speech to be heard twice as fast. Since the final scaling is applied to the result of applying user-defined audio-rendering rules, the relative changes in state effected by rendering rules are preserved.

AFL Expressions

We now define AFL expressions that yield a new speech state —these have no side-effects. The simplest expressions are the names of the nine predefined voices (e.g., *afl:paul*) and the names of variables to which states have been assigned. Using these expressions to move in the speech space makes the space a collection of discrete points. In addition, AFL provides four operators for generating new points in speech space. Each of these "move operators" expresses a change along a single dimension of the state space. While one move operator would have been sufficient, having multiple operators makes AFL easier to use. These operators allow us to express relative changes to the speech state. To give some intuition, they provide the same ability as scaling a font in the visual setting.

Expression

(move-by <point> <dimension> <offset>*)*

yields a state that is the same as *<point>* except that *<offset>* has been added to dimension *<dimension>*. For example, the following statement adds 50% to the assertiveness of *'afl:paul.*

(move-by 'afl:paul afl:assertiveness 50)

Expression

(scale-by <point> <dimension> <factor>*)*

yields a new state, *<point>* with the value of dimension *<dimension>* multiplied by *<factor>*.

Expression

(*move-to <point> <dimension> <value>*)

yields state *<point>* with the value of dimension *<dimension>* set to *<value>*.

Expression

(step-by <point> <dimension> <steps>*)*

yields state <*point*> with the value for dimension <*dimension*> changed by <*steps*> steps. Each dimension has a default step size, which specifies the minimum change needed to be perceptible. The step sizes for the MultiVoice parameters are shown in the "step size" column of Table 3.1. Using *step-by*, one can have the value of a dimension changed by a multiple of the step size.

The step-size for a particular dimension can also be changed by supplying the additional keyword *afl:step-size* to any of the AFL operators. For example, while the expression

(afl:step-by afl:average-pitch -1.5)

yields a new state with the value of *afl:average-pitch* changed, the expression

(*afl:move-by afl:average-pitch* 2 *:slot afl:step-size*)

yields a new state with the step size for *afl:average-pitch* changed to 2. Note that this expression makes use of named parameters in *Common Lisp*.

The four move operators are shown in their simple form. In general, these operators take a point and a list of dimension-value pairs specifying how to move.

(<*operator*> <*point*> ((<dim_1> <val_1>) $\cdots$ (<dim_n> <val_n>)))

Summary of the Speech Component

Table 3.2 summarizes the speech generation statements provided by the speech component.

Table 3.2. AFL statements for generating speech events.

Statement	Description
(*send-text* <*text*>)	Send text.
(*speak-number* <*number*>)	Speak number.
(*force-speech*)	Force speech.
(*pause* <*msec*>)	Insert silence.
(*subclause-boundary*)	Clause boundary.
(*comma-intonation*)	Comma intonation.
(*exclamation*)	exclamation intonation.
(*interrogative*)	Interrogative intonation.
(*high-intonation*)	Rising intonation.
(*low-intonation*)	Falling intonation.
(*high-low-intonation*)	Rise and fall.
(*primary-stress*)	Primary stress.
(*secondary-stress*)	Secondary stress.
(*exclamatory-stress*)	Exclamatory stress.

The intonational markers we use correspond to the description in [Pie81]. Note however, that MultiVoice does not provide all of the intonational markers described therein —see Chapter 5 of the MultiVoice reference manual [Tec91] for a detailed discussion on intonational markers on MultiVoice.

To conclude this section, here is a summary of the rest of the statements provided by the speech component. Many of these statements will be extended to work in other component spaces in the next section.

- **Variable:** **current-speech-state**
  Contains the current speech state.
- **Variable:** **global-speech-state**
  Contains the global speech state.
- **Statement:** (*local-set-state <point>*)
  Assign value of *<point>* to **current-speech-state**.
- **Statement:** (*global-set-state <point>*)
  Assign the value of *<point>* to **global-speech-state**.
- **Operator:** (*<op> <pt> <dim> <val>*)
  Return the state reached by *moving* along *<dim>* by *<val>* from *<pt>*. The type of move is specified by *<op>* where

$$\langle op \rangle \in \{\textit{move-by},\ \textit{move-to},\ \textit{scale-by},\ \textit{step-by}\}$$

- **Operator:** (*gen-op <pt> '(<op> <dim> <val>)* ⋯) Provides the functionality of all the other operators.
- **Statement:** (*set-final-scale-factor <dim> <factor>*)
  assign *<factor>* as the final scale factor for *<dim>*.
- **Statement:** (*initialize-speech-space*)
  Initialize current and global speech state.

Using Common Lisp

Thus far, we have described the parts of AFL that deal directly with manipulating the speech state. Remember, however, that AFL is implemented on top of *Common Lisp*, so all *Common Lisp* statements may be used when writing AFL program segments. *Common Lisp* has conditional statements, loops, recursion, etc., so the full power of a conventional language is available. Naturally, were the audio-rendering system to be implemented on another programming platform, AFL would have to be fleshed out to include general programming-language statements.

3.3 Combining Different Spaces in AFL

In general, the output device may consist of any number of speech and nonspeech components, each of which is a named component of the audio formatter. Individual components provide operators for moving in the space, etc., as described in the sections on the individual component spaces. In this section, we describe how these component spaces are combined to form the total audio space. The AFL block and assignment statements, which have been described in the context of a single component, will now be extended to work in the total audio space.

States in AFL

Conceptually, AFL maintains one local and one global state in program variables **current-total-audio-state** and **global-total-audio-state**. Since it is easier to think of speech and non-speech audio separately, we treat these as named component subspaces with their own state variables. Thus, variables **global-speech-state** and **current-speech-state** are really components of these states, so that the fully qualified references to these variables are

global-total-audio-state*. *global-speech-state

and

current-total-audio-state*. *current-speech-state

The names of these fields provide the external interface to the individual components.

We now describe how components are combined to form the *total audio space*. The AFL block is now extended to work in the total audio space; it introduces a local variable **current-...** for each of the components.

Assignment statements

(local-set-state <point>*)*

and

(global-set-state <point>*)*

assign the value of expression *<point>* to AFL state variables. The type of *<point>* determines the component state variable that will be set. Hence, if there are several component spaces of a given type, e.g., several speech components, the fully qualified name of the state variable must also be given, as in

(*local-set-state <point> *current-speech-state**)

AFL assignment statements are implemented as generic functions. The space-specific methods on the assignment statements perform the following steps:

1. Synchronize actions as necessary for this component space.
2. Set the variable that encapsulates the state of this component space to the value of the expression that is supplied.
3. Call the hardware specific *set-state* function.

Adding a component space requires some work but can be done easily by someone familiar with the implementation. To add a new component space:

1. Define the space and build the underlying implementation.
2. Define the external interface by providing state variables.
3. Provide the space-specific methods on the assignment statements.

Synchronization

The various components of an audio formatter can have separate threads of control. AFL constructs are needed to synchronize events occurring on these multiple components. The AFL block serves as a *cobegin* statement; a block terminates only after all events started within it have been completed. We now address issues that come up in designing the AFL block as a *cobegin* statement.

In a typical audio formatter having a speech and sound component, we may specify that a sound is to play repeatedly on the sound component while certain actions are executing on the speech component. The AFL block should not terminate until speech commenced from inside that block has completed —otherwise the sound will be turned off prematurely in this example. Invariably, with any speech synthesizer, the speech will fall far behind the host computer that is generating the text to be spoken. One way to avoid this is to synthesize a word at a time and wait till it has been spoken, but then all intonation is lost. Text must be sent in large enough chunks so that intonational cues are retained. This means that events on other component spaces have to be explicitly synchronized with speech space events. The AFL block, by serving as a *cobegin* statement, abstracts these details from an AFL program.

AFL events are of two types:

1. Simple events that execute an action once. Such events are executed by statements like *send-text*.
2. Events that repeatedly execute an action. These are executed within an implicit *loop forever* statement. The actions executed within the *loop forever* statement are typically simple events.

An AFL block terminates only after all simple events commenced within that block have terminated. Components executing events of the second type (within a *loop forever* construct) are said to be *busy*. AFL blocks keep track of *busy* components, and when a block terminates, all events of the second type commenced within that block are aborted.

Note that any event on an audio component terminates in the AFL block in which it was begun. It is not possible to begin an event in one block and have the block terminate but let the event continue. Upon first glance, this restriction may seem too strong. However, in many experiments with ASTER, AFL has proven to be sufficiently expressive. Further, this restriction tremendously simplifies the semantics of the AFL language and its implementation.

Tracking Busy Components

To preserve the scope rules of AFL, two tables are used to record busy components. Table *busy-table*, with global scope, has one entry for each component, and all its entries are initially *false*. When a *loop forever* event is started on a component, the corresponding entry in *busy-table* is set to *true*. Once a component has become busy, no other events can be executed on it; but its current state can be changed, e.g., the pitch of the sound that is playing on a busy component could be changed.

When a block terminates, only *loop forever* events commenced inside that block are aborted. To implement this, we introduce table *local-busy-table* with an entry for each component. This table is local to the AFL block, and all its entries are initialized to *false*. When terminating a block, entries in the local copy of *local-busy-table* are checked to determine the components whose *loop forever* events are to be aborted.

Thus, when terminating a block, the following steps are performed in sequence:

1. Wait for completion of events on components whose *busy-table* entry is *false*.
2. Abort ongoing events on components whose entry in the *local-busy-table* is *true*.

3.4 Audio Formatting using Non-Speech Audio

This section describes the design and implementation of the *sound* component of the audio formatter. AFL variables **current-audio-state** and **global-audio-state** represent the local and global states of this component. Here, *state* is a point in *sound space*. The sound component provides operators for constructing new points. AFL assignment statements can be used to set the local and global states of the sound component in a manner similar to that described in the case of the speech component. The local scope introduced by AFL blocks also applies to **current-audio-state**.

Space of Sound Cues

We define the space of sound cues just as we defined the speech space. Things are a little more complicated in this case, because it is not so clear what all the dimensions are, or even whether the number of dimensions is finite. If by non-speech audio we mean any audible sound different from intelligible speech, the space is indeed very large. In order to use non-speech audio effectively, we need to restrict the space. Thus, in the following, the sound space is a suitably restricted subspace of the entire space of non-speech audio.

The following enumerates a few of the dimensions we could use in constructing the non-speech component. Depending on the type of hardware available, we will have fewer or more dimensions.

1. Amplitude of sound.
2. Pitch (fundamental frequency).
3. Frequency of the different harmonics.
4. Attenuation or resonance.
5. Directionality.

We thus think of a point in this restricted subspace of non-speech audio as a distinct sound. Each channel of audio output is a point in an instance of such a subspace. Multiple channels of sound are thus modeled as a direct sum of these subspaces.

In the following, the sound space and the associated primitives for working in this space are defined assuming no restrictions on the underlying hardware. However, ASTER restricts itself to the simpler setting provided by SPARC audio.

Types of Operators

The operators for moving in sound space are similar to those of the speech space (see Sec. 3.2). The distinguishing factor here is that sounds have duration, so the duration needs to be specified. This either takes the form of a simple time unit or is specified in terms of synchronizing the non-speech audio with events on other components, e.g., "play this sound until a particular event has completed". As discussed in Sec. 3.3, the AFL block serves as the smallest unit of synchronization.

Synchronize and Play. Primitive *play-once* waits until pending events on all audio components have finished executing before itself executing the event specified by the current point in sound-space. The action executed by *play-once* could itself be either synchronous or asynchronous. In either case, the duration of the event is specified explicitly as a time unit or implicitly by the nature of the event. Primitive *synchronize-and-play* is similar, except that the sound to be played is specified explicitly.

ASTER typically uses this primitive to generate sounds to cue the beginning of the rendering of certain objects.

Play until Told to Stop. Another type of synchronization primitive specifies that an event is to be repeated until certain other events occur. Thus, we can specify that a certain sound-space event is to be repeated for the duration of the rendering of an object. Here, the duration of the event is specified in terms of other events taking place in the audio formatter. We can picture this as turning on a conceptual switch on the *audio player* and turning it off at a later time. This is achieved by executing a *loop-forever* statement, as discussed in Sec. 3.3; such an event is terminated when the block in which it appears is ready to terminate.

Select a Sound to Play. In an implementation where we can actually move along all the dimensions in the sound space, the new state would be specified using move operators. However, in a more primitive implementation environment where this is not possible, selecting a sound or moving to a new state amounts to picking one of a set of distinguished points. Thus, the space becomes discrete.

Examples of Use

Here are some examples of the use of non-speech audio cues in ASTER.

The following rendering rule for itemized lists uses a sound cue to denote an "audio bullet", with the sound cue being played before rendering each item of the list. The synchronization provided by *play-once* ensures that the sound cue for each item in the list is played only after the text from the previous item has been spoken.

```
(def-reading-rule...
    (afl:new-block (loop  for item in items  do
                          (afl:synchronize-and-play
                               *item-cue*)
                          (read-aloud item))))
```

An *audio highlight* is a sound that repeats in the background while text is being spoken. The rendering rule given below *audio highlights* the abstract in a technical document using the non-speech primitives. The rule locally selects a sound and turns on the non-speech audio. This results in the sound repeating in the background. Since this action of turning on the audio is executed within the block commenced in the rendering rule for the abstract, the sound is automatically turned off once the abstract has been spoken. Further, since the AFL block is an implicit cobegin statement, it terminates only after all speech activity commenced inside the block have been completed —as a consequence the audio highlight is turned off only after the entire abstract has been spoken.

```
(def-reading-rule ...
    (afl:new-block
     (afl:local-set-state
      (afl:select-sound afl:*current-audio-state* *abs-cue*))
     (afl:local-set-state
      (afl:switch-on afl:*current-audio-state*)) ...))
```

Implementation Details

The following constraints are imposed by the implementation environment:

1. ASTER currently uses only digitized sounds. The non-speech space is therefore discrete.
2. Sparc audio allows only one channel of output, since there is only one sound chip.

The current implementation of non-speech audio uses the Lucid multitasking facility. It also uses the Lucid extensions to *Common Lisp* for interfacing with existing *UNIX* utilities and programs written in *C*.

Audio Player. Object *audio-player* provides an abstraction barrier between the external interface to the sound space and the underlying implementation —the interface only deals with object *audio-player*. An *audio-player* consists of a *sound* to be played, a *function* to play the sound and a *switch* to turn the sound on and off. Once an audio player object has been created, its sound can be changed, and it can also be turned on and off using its switch. The external interface to the sound space maps points to the state of the underlying audio player. We can think of object *audio-player* as the underlying hardware for the sound component of the audio space. Thus, we could have one audio-player for each audio component. Object *audio-player* is implemented so as to allow the use of other sound generation software that becomes available in the future. Given a function f that generates sound when called with argument s, we can create an audio player with function f and sound s to create a uniform interface to the underlying sound generation software.

AFL blocks and assignments are used to manipulate the external representation of the state of the subspace, and the underlying hardware representation, in this case the *audio-player*, is automatically updated.

Using other Sound Generation Tools. Object *audio-player* allows the use of other sound generation tools with little modification to the AFL primitives.

PLAY-NOTES is a simple C program that plays a short beep when called with a set of arguments. A foreign function interface to this C function provides the *Lisp* counterpart:

```
(play-notes &key(volume length tone decay octave))
```

To create an audio player that uses the above to generate sounds, we can write:

```
(setf *play-notes*
      (make-instance 'audio-player :function #'play-notes
                                   :sound (list :octave "5c" )))
```

We can now turn this object on or off, and also change the note that is played by executing:

```
(setf (player-sound *play-notes* )
      (list :octave "6c"))
```

Finally, we can implement a new component space around this audio-player object, called the *play-notes-space*, with its local state etc., and manipulate it using AFL constructs.

3.5 The Pronunciation Component

The pronunciation of a word depends on the type of text being spoken. For instance, when speaking mathematics, it is important to say "cap gamma" when rendering Γ, whereas when rendering plain text, upper case is not significant. Similarly, if an English document contains French phrases, these should be pronounced according to French pronunciation rules.

We model pronunciation as a separate component of the audio formatter. The corresponding state space is discrete, with points representing different pronunciation modes. Notice that the pronunciation component does not correspond to a separate hardware component of the audio formatter.

Example of Use

Consider a document that describes the career of the French mathematician Galois. The introduction might read:

> The works of Galois were, as we know, published in 1846 by Liouville, in the *Journal de Mathématiques*. It is unfortunate that we do not have the works of the great geometer as an isolated body; thus, the *Société mathématique* decided to reprint Galois' papers.

Speaking this using pronunciation rules of English results in poor audio formatting. However, if the French phrases are clearly marked up, as in

```
\french{Soci\'et\'e math\'ematique}
```

we can write a rendering rule for object *french* (See Sec. 2.4 for details on new objects) as follows:

```
(defmethod read-aloud ((object french))
  "Render a french phrase. "
  (afl:new-block (afl:local-set-state :french)
                 (read-aloud (argument 1 object ))))
```

This results in the French phrases being pronounced correctly.

In our implementation, the effect of executing *(afl:local-set-state :french)* is to change the internal pronunciation table that is consulted before pronouncing a word —if the pronunciation for a phrase is not defined in this table, then the word will be mispronounced. In speaking French phrases, this is only an intermediate solution; to truly speak a different language, we need a multilingual speech synthesizer. However, AFL programs remain the same, no matter what the underlying implementation and hardware.

3.6 Some Concluding Remarks on AFL

The Simplicity of the AFL Block

In conventional programming languages, the block is used to introduce local variables, whose names and types are chosen by the programmer. In AFL, however, the block is used only to introduce a fixed set of local variables, each of which is associated with the current state of one component of the audio formatter.

The main advantage we gain from having a restricted block is simplicity of semantics and implementation. The hardware for each audio component is associated with a particular variable. The contents of the variable can be changed only through an explicit assignment to the variable, so it is not difficult in the implementation to change the hardware when the variable is assigned. AFL is optimized so that only those dimensions that are actually changed have to be conveyed to the hardware. Further, the particular variable that is associated with the hardware can be switched only by the beginning and end of execution of a block. Hence, the implementation of the change of association is simple.

The use of the restricted block leads to the rule that any audio event that is begun in a block must end in that block. In all our extensive experimentation and experience with AsTeR, we have not found this rule to be an inconvenience. In fact, we have been helped by the imposed discipline. On the other hand, taking advantage of a more flexible block (were it available) would only complicate the structure and interaction of various rendering rules, in much the same way that the goto can cause undue complications in conventional programming languages.

Consider, for example, rendering rules of the following form:

- A rendering rule for fractions that plays a sound when speaking the numerator and denominator.
- A rendering rule for superscripts that turns off the non-speech audio without first declaring a local non-speech audio state.

When rendering a fraction whose numerator is a superscripted variable, e.g., $\frac{x^2}{y+1}$, the above would result in the sound getting turned off by the superscript rendering rule, and this effect would persist for the rest of the rendering of the fraction. Since rendering rules are written for specific object types, many of which can be nested, the above kind of bug would become common if component states were not local to every block.

External and Internal Direct Sums

To give a slightly different intuition, there are two *views* of a vector space formed by the direct sum of component spaces. These views are isomorphic when the space is considered as an algebraic entity. In the internal view, the space is made up of several subspaces that we see as individual components. The components are entities in themselves and can be directly manipulated. This is the view taken by conventional block structured languages. No local copies of state variables are made automatically. The block is *internal* to the state space.

In the external view, the vector space is a single entity having different components, and it is this latter view that AFL blocks have of the total audio space. Blocks are external to the state space, so whenever a new block is executed, the local state is a copy of the current point in the total space. This means that local copies are made of all the component states.

Benefits of AFL

The benefits of ASTER, which is based on AFL, cannot be experienced by reading a printed document such as this; rather, one has to listen to ASTER in action. Suffice it to say that ASTER has made it possible for the author to read current technical material, on his own, that otherwise would not have been available for years (if at all). Further, he can tune the renderings (see Chap. 4) to his liking and can even browse the document. Thus, AFL represents a gigantic step forward in providing the tools necessary to render technical documents in audio.

Several further points can be made.

- AFL provides for audio renderings the same power that TEX provides for visual renderings. AFL has made it possible for us to experiment easily and quickly with different audio renderings of mathematical notations. In this regard, we are limited only by our own ability to think of new ways of rendering mathematics clearly and succinctly; the language itself is not the limitation.
- As a result of its focus on multiple components, AFL is an extensible tool for writing high-level programs for producing multimodal renderings of information. While it is not trivial to design and implement a new audio component, it also need not be a long and laborious affair. Based on the author's experience, we guess that it would take him less than a week to add a new component that is based on a different speech synthesizer or sound component.

4. Rendering Rules and Styles

We begin this chapter by building up a general framework of rendering rules and styles in Sec. 4.1. Rendering rules enable the generation of different audio views of the same object. Sec. 4.2 introduces the concept of fleeting and persistent sound cues and uses these to develop an audio layout for conveying structure present in typical document content, e.g., sections and itemized lists.

We then develop a system of audio notation to convey mathematical content and present a collection of rendering rules for producing such audio notation in Sec. 4.3. The processing required to produce context sensitive renderings from the quasi-prefix representation (see Chap. 2.2) is covered in Sec. 4.4. Some descriptive rendering rules for mathematical content are discussed in Sec. 4.5.

When reading complex mathematics in print, we often use a chunking strategy: rather than read the entire expression, we first obtain a high-level view by grouping related subexpressions. This becomes even more necessary in oral communication —otherwise, the listener has to remember the mathematical content. Complicated mathematical expressions can be better communicated by first substituting names for complex subexpressions to provide a quick overview. This process, called rendering with *variable substitution*, is described in Sec. 4.6. A flexible mechanism for delaying the rendering of specific objects is described in Sec. 4.7. App. A.4 documents the external interface to the system of rendering rules and styles.

Throughout this chapter, we describe how AsTeR renders different object types. Note, however, that the user is free to customize all of the renderings produced by AsTeR.

4.1 Rendering Rules and Styles

AsTeR renders document objects by calling generic function *read-aloud.* Primary methods[1] can be defined on this function for objects that appear in the document model described in Sec. 2.1.

[1] We use standard method combination as defined in *CLOS.* See App. A.6 for an overview of some of these terms.

The body of such a *read-aloud* method consists of AFL statements that set AFL state and execute audio events. For instance, the *read-aloud* method for object *string* is:

```
(defmethod read-aloud ((text string))
  "Render a string."
  (afl:send-text text))
```

Here is a slightly more complex example:

```
(defmethod read-aloud ((article article ))
  "Abbreviated read-aloud method for article. "
  (when (title article) (read-aloud  (title article )))
  (read-aloud (body article)))
```

Function *read-aloud*, as described so far, can produce only one view of a document —it can render it in only one way. To enable different views of the same object, we now introduce the notion of rendering rules and styles. This makes function *read-aloud* more involved.

A rendering rule associates a name with a set of actions that are to be executed when an instance of a given object type is rendered. The format of a rendering rule is

(*def-reading-rule* (<*object-name*> <*rule-name*>) <*afl statements*>)

The body of the rule consists of AFL statements that modify AFL state and execute audio events —it is the same as the body of an instance of method *read-aloud*.

Named rendering rules permit the user to define several rules for the same object, but now, a mechanism is needed to determine which rule to use when rendering instances of an object O. At any time, only one rendering rule is *active* for object O, and this active rule is used by *read-aloud*.

Rules can be activated and deactivated interactively by executing

(*activate-rule* <*object-name*> <*rule-name*>)

and

(*deactivate-rule* <*object-name*>)

Each rule presents a different audio view of the object. AsTeR provides a collection of default rendering rules (in the form of primary methods on *read-aloud*) that are used when no rule has been explicitly activated for a particular object type.

Within the body of a rendering rule, we recommend that sub-objects be rendered only by calling function *read-aloud*. This ensures that if a listener activates a new rendering rule for an object O, then all instances of O will be rendered using this rule. For example, after activating a rendering rule for fractions, a summation that contains a fraction as the summand gets rendered as expected, i.e., the summation is rendered as before, but the fraction in the summand is rendered using the newly activated rule. Of course, a rendering rule is free to activate and deactivate other rules. Note, however, that this will hard-wire a particular type of rendering into such a rule.

Rendering Styles

Activating rendering rules provides a convenient mechanism for obtaining different views of a single object type. However, this is cumbersome when changing how several object types are rendered —we will have to explicitly activate a different rule for each object type. This is obviated by the introduction of *rendering styles.*

A rendering style *style-1* is the collection of rendering rules named *style-1*, each of which renders a different object type. ASTER maintains a list of active styles in the order in which they were activated. Initially, this list contains only style *default*, which specifies a default rendering for all objects.

The user can execute

(*activate-style style-1*)

to add *style-1* to the front of the list of active styles. This effectively activates all rules that appear in *style-1* —when rendering an object, ASTER uses the most recently activated style that defines a rule for that object.

Style *style-1* can be deactivated by executing

(*deactivate-style style-1*)

A listener can create a new rendering style simply by defining rendering rules for one or more object types. The style need not provide rules for all the known object types —rules for the remaining objects are taken from previously active styles. Thus, we might define rules in style *descriptive* for summations, integrals and coproducts. If *descriptive* is now activated, and style *simple* is the next most-recently activated style, ASTER uses rendering rules from *simple* for all other objects. Typically, the list of active styles is:

```
(use-special-patterns descriptive simple default)
```

If no rule has been explicitly activated for an object type O, then the active rule for O is provided by the most recently activated style that defines a rendering rule for O or one of its superclasses. Thus, in the above example, if the list of active styles is *descriptive, simple, default*, the active rule for an integral is *descriptive.* If we now want to have all objects rendered using this list of active styles but would like integrals rendered using rule *simple*, then we would execute

(*activate-rule 'integral 'simple*)

The ability to obtain different views of an object is a very useful learning aid. It gives the listener a chance to obtain different perspectives of complex expressions. Further, this system of rendering rules and styles has proven very useful in experimenting with different ways of rendering mathematics.

Rendering rules can be used in many interesting ways. For instance, defining and activating the following rule for paragraphs provides a thumb-nail view of a document.

```
(def-reading-rule (paragraph quiet) nil)
```

The body of this rule is empty, so the contents of paragraphs are not rendered. When this rule is activated, only the titles of the sectional units will be spoken.

```
(def-reading-rule (paragraph read-only-display-math)
    "Render only  the math appearing in paragraphs"
  (let ((math-in-paragraph
        (mapcar #'(lambda(object)
                    (when  (display-math-p object) object))
                (contents paragraph ))))
    (mapc #'read-aloud  math-in-paragraph)))
```

Fig. 4.1. Rendering only displayed math.

The rendering rule in Fig. 4.1 renders only the displayed math from a document. Activating this rule allows the listener to locate an equation of interest quickly. The user can now reactivate the normal rendering rule for paragraphs and listen to the entire paragraph that contains the math expression. This is like flicking through the pages of a book until something of interest is located and then reading the relevant content.

4.2 Rendering Document Content

Document structure is implicitly conveyed in audio renderings by using audio layout made up of extra-textual speech and non-speech audio cues. The following subsections describe this audio layout and outline the rules for producing such renderings from the internal representation described in Sec. 2.1.

Audio cues are either *fleeting* or *persistent*. This classification is orthogonal to the earlier classification into speech and non-speech audio cues. We define terms *fleeting* and *persistent* below:

Definition 4.2.1. *Fleeting cue:*
A cue that does not last. Such cues are characterized by their duration being specified by the nature of the cue itself.

Definition 4.2.2. *Persistent cue:*
A cue that lasts, i.e., persists. The duration for such cues is specified by other ongoing events in the audio rendering, rather than by the cue itself.

The following paragraphs clarify the above definitions by giving some examples of fleeting and persistent cues.

Examples of fleeting cues

- Speech: Announce[2] "title" before speaking the title.
- Non-speech: Play a short sound to indicate a bullet when rendering itemized lists.

AsTeR minimizes the use of extra-textual announcements by cueing document structure implicitly wherever possible. Fleeting sound cues are associated with objects like paragraphs and bulletted lists to convey structure efficiently. To give a visual analogy, we all know what a table of numbers or a centered paragraph look like, but what do they "sound" like? Associating sound cues (earcons [BGB88]) with specific structures takes a step towards answering this question.

Fleeting cues are typically used to introduce particular objects. However, more than an introductory cue is needed when rendering complex structures. For instance, a fleeting cue at the beginning of each item is not sufficient when rendering an itemized list —the listener is likely to forget the current context if the items are complex.

In the visual setting, the logical structure of a list is displayed by superimposing indentation, an implicit layout cue, on the text. AsTeR uses persistent audio cues to achieve a similar effect. These cues consist of either a change in some characteristic of the speaking voice or a sound that repeats in the background and have the advantage of being present during the entire rendering, without detracting from the flow of information.

Examples of persistent cues

- Speech: Raise the pitch of the voice when rendering the contents of an itemized list.
- Non-speech: Play a continuously repeating sound while speaking an abstract.

Audio layout Audio layout is achieved by super-imposing fleeting and persistent cues on the rendering. To convey nesting effectively, the AFL state changes used to achieve persistent cues need to be monotonic in the mathematical sense. Let P represent a point in audio space. Let f be a change-of-state function. To convey nesting effectively, f should be monotonic —there should exist an ordering

$$P < f(P) < f^2(P) < \cdots \tag{4.1}$$

where this ordering is perceptible. This is where we exploit the abstraction of a speech space and the operators it provides. For instance, the following AFL

[2] All fleeting speech cues are verbalized using a slightly softer voice to set them apart from actual document content.

statement can be used to define a function that generates new AFL states for rendering itemized lists:

```
(afl:step-by afl:*current-speech-state*  'afl:average-pitch 1)
```

This notion of monotonicity in change of AFL states will be exploited once again in Sec. 4.3 when designing an audio notation for mathematics.

Rendering Hierarchical Document Objects

The rendering rule for different sectioning levels uses a fleeting speech cue by announcing the current level, e.g., "section", announcing positional information, e.g., section number, and then speaking the title of the sectional unit. A persistent sound cues the title —it is "highlighted" by playing a sound in the background. Here is the corresponding rendering rule:

```
(def-reading-rule (section default)
    "Render section"
     (afl:new-block
          (afl:local-set-state
               (afl:step-by afl:*current-speech-state*
                    'afl:smoothness 2))
          (read-aloud (section-name section))
          (read-aloud (section-number section)))
     (afl:new-block
          (afl:local-set-state
               (afl:step-by  afl:*current-speech-state*
                    'afl:head-size 1))
          (afl:local-set-state
               (afl:select-sound afl:*current-audio-state*
                    *title-highlight*))
          (afl:local-set-state
               (afl:switch-on afl:*current-audio-state*))
          (read-aloud (section-title section)))
     ...);render body of section
```

Paragraphs are introduced by a fleeting sound:

```
(def-reading-rule (paragraph default)
    (afl:new-block
     (afl:synchronize-and-play *paragraph-cue*)
     (afl:paragraph-begin)                ;rising intonation.
     <render contents>))
```

Special environments. Lists, centered text and other structures are marked up in LaTeX as special environments and are characterized by their visual layout. Thus, a list of items is cued by indenting the items in the list. Nested lists are displayed by indenting them with respect to the outer list —in audio, we use change of pitch.

An itemized list is represented internally as an object of type *itemized-list*, with the list of items as its children. Each item itself can be a complex object. Here is the AFL rule for rendering object *itemized-list*.

```
(def-reading-rule (itemized-list default)
    (afl:new-block
     (afl:local-set-state
      (afl:step-by afl:*current-speech-state*
                   'afl:average-pitch 1))
     (loop for child in children do (read-aloud child))))
```

This rendering rule begins a block, locally sets the state of the audio formatter by raising the pitch of the voice, and then renders the contents of the itemized list. These contents are rendered relative to the containing list. When this rule is applied to a nested list, the inner list gets rendered relative to the outer list —the pitch goes up by one step when rendering the outer list, and goes up by another step when rendering the inner list. Thus, the local scope introduced by the AFL block works effectively in conveying nested structures.

Rendering tables. Just speaking the contents of a table does not convey the relation between its entries. Saying "next column" and "next row" before rendering each new row or column is too distracting. We overcome this problem by exploiting stereo (spatial audio). The first element of each row is spoken solely on the left speaker; the rendering then progressively moves to the right, with the last element spoken solely on the right speaker. Thus, given a row $(A_{k0}, A_{k1}, \ldots, A_{kn})$, element A_{ki} is spoken with the volume of the left speaker at $\frac{n-i}{n}$max-volume and the right volume at $\frac{i}{n}$max-volume.

We achieve this with a simple AFL rendering rule: the volume of the left and right speakers are dimensions in audio space, and implementing the above rendering only requires moving along the line spanned by these dimensions.

4.3 Rendering Mathematics

This section defines an *audio notation* for mathematics and presents rendering rules that produce this audio notation.

There is little similarity between developing a written notation and its audio counterpart. However, the evolution of written notation shows the following.

> Any notational system is a combination of conventions and an intuitive use of the various dimensions that are provided by the perceptual modality and the means available to produce output appropriate for that modality.

We use this insight to develop a concise audio notation for spoken mathematics that exploits the available audio dimensions. It is conceivable that the number of audio dimensions will increase with the improvement in the relevant technology, enabling more sophisticated notational systems in the future.

We characterize all of written mathematical notation as follows:

- Projects the inherent tree-structure present in mathematical expressions on to a two-dimensional display —different delimiters are used and mathematical expressions are stacked above one another.
- Annotates this tree structure with visual attributes. We identify six attributes that use different aspects of the two-dimensional display —changes in baseline and changes in font size— see Fig. 2.1.

The visual cues used to project the tree structure are independent of the cues used to produce the attributes. Hence, attributes may themselves contain arbitrarily complex tree structures. Thus, conventional mathematical notation uses a consistent set of visual layout primitives to construct complex displays.

Written notation provides the ability to render mathematical objects without understanding their meaning. The underlying structure can be recreated by a reader familiar with the subject matter at hand and the notational system in use. Internalizing and browsing this structure is helped by the use of different types of visual delimiters such as (, [, {, |, $\underbrace{\quad}$ and $\overbrace{\quad}$ —these help the author mark off "interesting" subtrees within an expression.

In contrast, plain spoken renderings of mathematical expressions are completely linear, thereby losing much of this expressive power. Spoken descriptions of complex mathematics (found on talking books) compensate for this loss of expressive power by using extra-textual phrases, thereby making the renderings verbose.

To overcome these problems, we develop an equivalent *audio notation.* The first step is to identify dimensions in the audio space to parallel the functionality of the dimensions in the visual setting. The second step is to augment these audio dimensions with the use of pauses, intonational cues such as voice inflection, and descriptive phrases.

AsTeR implements this notational system by using fleeting and persistent cues, especially by exploiting the computer's ability to vary the characteristics of a synthetic voice. Renderings produced are therefore much more concise.

Our audio notation minimizes the verbiage in math renderings. Concise renderings serve to convey the concepts involved succinctly, leaving the listener time to reason about the expression. More descriptive renderings (with explanatory phrases to cue structure) can be used when listening to unfamiliar material. Thus, there is a wide range of possible renderings of a math expression varying between fully descriptive and completely notational. The choice of how much to rely on the audio notation, and how descriptive renderings should be, is entirely subjective.

Here are the features we require of our audio notation for mathematics:

- Produce concise renderings: Avoid detracting from the mathematical content by using as few extra-textual phrases as possible.

- Convey nested structures: The notation conveys deeply nested structures, such as a subscript in a superscript, and complex subexpressions appearing as subscripts or superscripts.
- Convey context: The renderings convey as much context as possible without adding to the verbiage.

Producing Audio Notation for Mathematics

We exploit the abstraction of the audio space to define unique audio dimensions that make up the various pieces of the notation. These dimensions can be thought of as lines[3] determined by a combination of the speech and non-speech dimensions described in Chap. 3. The AFL states used to produce different pieces of the audio notation are reached by "moving" along these dimensions. The functions used to generate new states are monotonic in the mathematical sense described in 4.1.

We choose unique audio dimensions to map the quasi-prefix form into audio space. The quasi-prefix representation is a tree with attributes. We pick one audio dimension, denoted by *dim-children* (see Fig. 4.2), along which to vary the current AFL state as different levels of a tree are rendered. We next choose dimensions orthogonal to *dim-children* to cue the visual attributes as follows. Let x and y denote two speech-space dimensions that are orthogonal to *dim-children*. Select three lines in the speech space, $x = 0$, $x + y = 0$, and $x - y = 0$. Moving forward or backward along these three lines cues the six visual attributes.

Conventional mathematical notation has built up a strong association between the superscript and subscript, in that we intuitively think of them as opposites, i.e., the superscript moves up, and the subscript moves down. AsTeR takes advantage of this association by moving the AFL state "forward" along the line $x - y = 0$ before rendering superscripts and "backward" along this same line before rendering subscripts. States along the line $x + y = 0$ cue left superscripts and subscripts; states along $x = 0$ cue accents and underbars. By our choice of x and y, these variations are independent of dimension *dim-children*. See Fig. 4.3 and Fig. 4.4 for the audio dimensions that are currently used for cueing superscripting and subscripting.

```
(afl:multi-step-by state
   '(afl:smoothness 2) '(afl:richness -1)   ;softer
   '(afl:loudness 2) '(afl:quickness 1) ;animated
   '(afl:hat-rise 2) '(afl:stress-rise 2)) ;animated
```

Fig. 4.2. Audio dimension used for rendering subtrees.

The effect of moving along the audio dimension shown in Fig. 4.2 is to produce a softer, more animated voice. As deeper levels of nesting are entered,

[3] In general, these may be curves rather than straight lines.

the change in voice characteristic produces a sense of falling off into the distance. A change along the audio dimension shown in Fig. 4.3 produces

```
(afl:generalized-afl-operator  state
   '(afl:step-by afl:average-pitch 1.5)
   '(afl:step-by afl:head-size -.5)
   '(afl:scale-by  afl:average-pitch .5 :slot afl:step-size)
   '(afl:scale-by afl:head-size .5 :slot afl:step-size))
```

Fig. 4.3. Audio dimension used for rendering superscripts.

a higher pitched voice. The change in the head size keeps the voice from sounding unpleasant. The step size along both the average-pitch and head-size dimensions are reduced. This allows unambiguous rendering of subscripts in superscripts. The change in AFL state in Fig. 4.4 is the exact opposite of the change in Fig. 4.3.

```
(afl:generalized-afl-operator state
   '(afl:step-by afl:average-pitch -1.5)
   '(afl:step-by afl:head-size .5)
   '(afl:scale-by  afl:average-pitch .5 :slot afl:step-size)
   '(afl:scale-by afl:head-size .5 :slot afl:step-size))
```

Fig. 4.4. Audio dimension used for rendering subscripts.

In cases where no contextual information is available, the visual attributes appearing on a math object are rendered in the following order:

1. Subscript.
2. Superscript.
3. Underbar.
4. Accent.
5. Left-subscript.
6. Left-superscript.

The above ordering is motivated by the fact that in traditional mathematical notation, the subscript binds[4] the tightest. The order in which attributes are rendered is encapsulated in *Lisp* variable **attributes-reading-order** and may be changed by a user.

In style *simple*, a commonly used rendering style, subscripts and superscripts are rendered by first moving either backwards or forwards along the audio dimensions shown in Fig. 4.3 and Fig. 4.4. This produces extremely concise and unambiguous renderings. Consider the following expressions:

[4] This is an unwritten rule, however, and may be different in some fields, though we do not know of one.

$$e^{e^{e^{x}}} e^{e^{x}} e^{x} \tag{4.2}$$

$$x + y^{\frac{2}{k+1}} \tag{4.3}$$

Here, a plain verbal rendering produces an unnecessarily complicated description that makes it difficult to comprehend the inherent structure present in the expression.

Here is an example to illustrate the benefits of an audio notation when rendering unusual mathematical notation. In the following, $+_n$ denotes addition modulo n. Given this information,

$$x +_n y +_n z$$

could be spoken as "x plus mod n y plus mod n z". However, if this information is unavailable, AsTeR can still produce a rendering that can be correctly interpreted by a listener who is aware of the fact that the + sign can be subscripted. Further, the listener who is familiar with $+_n$ denoting modulo arithmetic can now understand the expression.

In style *descriptive*, new AFL states are used only if necessary when rendering superscripts and subscripts. Typically, "x 1" in traditional spoken math means x_1. Rendering style *descriptive* takes advantage of this convention to avoid using new AFL states when rendering subscripts that are simple. Note, however, that by doing so, rendering style *descriptive* does introduce ambiguity in the renderings; x^{k1} and x^{k_1} will sound the same. In our experience, we have found that this ambiguity is not a problem when rendering mathematical texts; few authors write x^{k2} in place of the preferred x^{2k}.

Parenthesizing in audio. The technique used by written mathematical notation to cue tree structure is insufficient for audio renderings. Using a wide array of delimiters to write mathematics works, since the eye is able to quickly traverse the written formulae and pair off matching delimiters. The situation is slightly different in audio; merely announcing the delimiters as they appear is not enough —when listening to a delimited expression, the listener has to remember the enclosing delimiters. This insight was gained as a result of work in summer 91[5], when we implemented a prototype audio formatter for mathematical expressions. Fleeting sound cues (with the pitch conveying nesting level) were used to "display" mathematical delimiters, but deeply nested expressions were difficult to understand.

AsTeR enables a listener to keep track of the nesting level by using a persistent speech cue, achieved by moving along *dim-children*, when rendering the contents of a delimited expression. This, in combination with fleeting cues for signalling the enclosing delimiters, permits a listener to better comprehend deeply nested expressions. This is because the "nesting level information" is

[5] This is joint work with Dr. Dennis Arnon of Xerox PARC.

implicitly cued by the currently active voice (a persistent cue) used to render the parenthesized expression.

To give some intuition, we can think of different visual delimiters as introducing different "functional colors" at different subtrees of the expression. Using different AFL states to render the various subtrees introduces an equivalent "audio coloring". The structure imposed on the audio space by the AFL operators enables us to pick "audio colors" that introduce relative changes. This notion of *relative change* is vital in effectively conveying nested structures.

Mathematical expressions are spoken as infix or prefix depending on the operator and the currently active rendering style. The large operators such as $\int$, in addition to the mathematical functions like sin, are rendered as prefix. All other expressions are rendered as infix. A persistent speech cue indicates the nesting level —the AFL state is varied along audio dimension *dim-children* before rendering the children of an operator. The number of new states is minimized —complexity of math objects and precedence of mathematical operators determine if a new state is to be used (see Sec. 4.4 for details on the complexity measure used). Thus, while new AFL states are used when rendering the numerator and denominator of $\frac{a+b}{c+d}$, no new AFL state is introduced when rendering $\frac{a}{b}+c+d$. Similarly, when rendering $\sin x$, no new AFL state is used to speak x, but when rendering $\sin(x+y)$, a new AFL state is used to render the argument to sin.

In the context of rendering sub-expressions, introducing new AFL states can be thought of as parenthesizing in the visual context. In the light of this statement, the above assertion about minimizing AFL states can be interpreted as avoiding the use of unnecessary parentheses in the visual context. Thus, we write $a+bc+d$, rather than $a+(bc)+d$, but we use parentheses to write $(a+b)(c+d)$. Analogously, it is not necessary to introduce a new state for speaking the fraction when rendering $a+\frac{b}{c}+d$, whereas a new rendering state is introduced to speak the numerator and denominator of $\frac{a+b}{c+d}$.[6]

Dimension *dim-children* has been chosen to provide five to six unique points. This means that deeply nested structures such as continuous fractions are rendered unambiguously.

Consider the following example:

$$1+\cfrac{x}{1+\cfrac{x}{1+\cfrac{x}{1+\cfrac{x}{1+\cfrac{x}{1+\ddots}}}}} \tag{4.4}$$

Here, the voice drops by one step as each level of the continuous fraction is rendered. Since this effect is cumulative, the listener can perceive the deeply nested nature of the expression. The rendering rule for fractions is shown

[6] To see this, think of the fraction written linearly, i.e., $\frac{b}{c}=b/c$.

in Fig. 4.5. Notice that this rendering rule handles simple fractions differently. When rendering fractions of the form $\frac{a}{b}$, no new AFL states are used. In addition, there is a subtle verbal cue; when rendering simple fractions, AsTeR speaks "over" instead of "divided by". This distinction seems to make the renderings more effective, and in some of the informal tests we have carried out, listeners disambiguated between expressions using this distinction without even being aware of it.

```
(def-reading-rule (fraction simple)
    "simple rendering  rule for fractions "
  (let ((pause-amount  (compute-pause fraction ))
        (numerator (numerator-of fraction))
        (denominator (denominator-of fraction )))
    (read-aloud "fraction") (afl:comma-intonation)
    (afl:with-surrounding-pause pause-amount
      (cond
        ((and (leaf-p numerator)         ;simple fraction
              (leaf-p denominator))      ; form a /b
         (read-aloud numerator) (read-aloud "over" )
         (read-aloud denominator))
        (t (afl:new-block
            (afl:local-set-state         ; move along
             (reading-state 'dim-children)) ;dim-children
            (read-aloud numerator))
           (read-aloud  " divided by,  ") ;  old state
           (afl:new-block
            (afl:local-set-state         ; move along
             (reading-state 'dim-children)) ; dim-children
            (read-aloud denominator )))))))
```

where statement *(reading-state 'dim-children)* generates an AFL state along dimension *dim-children*, see Fig. 4.2.

Fig. 4.5. Rendering rule for fractions.

Using pauses. The audio dimensions are supplemented by using pauses around subexpressions to indicate grouping. The duration of the pause is based on the *weight* of a subexpression (See Sec. 4.4 for details on weight of an object, a complexity measure). If the weight of an object is 1, then no pause is inserted; otherwise the weight of the object is scaled by a constant factor given by **pause-around-child** to determine the number of milliseconds of pause to be inserted around the rendering.

Using the above, AsTeR speaks $a + \frac{b}{c} + d$ unambiguously by inserting a pause around the fraction. No pause is inserted in rendering the simple expression a, when it occurs by itself. Inserting a pause here is unnecessary and would have an adverse stuttering effect on the speech.

4.4 Processing the Quasi-Prefix Form

As described in Chap. 2, no semantic interpretation is attached to mathematical content at the recognition step. ASTER can be enhanced to recognize specialized notation and produce context-sensitive renderings (e.g., speak x^2 as "x squared"). Some context-specific processing is needed to produce such renderings, and this section outlines the kind of information that is available: the weight of an object and special patterns.

Measure *weight* quantifies the complexity of math expressions. The weight function is defined as follows:

1. The weight of a leaf node with attributes is 1 plus the sum of the weights of its attributes. Attributes are themselves math objects, and their weight is computed recursively.
2. The weight function on non-leaf nodes is defined recursively:

$$\begin{aligned}\text{weight}(m) &= \text{w-co} + \text{w-ch} + \text{w-at}\\ \text{w-co} &= \text{weight}(\text{contents}(m))\\ \text{w-ch} &= \text{weight}(\text{children}(m))\\ \text{w-at} &= \text{weight}(\text{attributes}(m))\end{aligned}$$

Recognizing Special Patterns

Recognizing special patterns makes renderings sound more natural. Consider how experienced readers speak math expressions. Even though $\frac{a+b}{c}$ is spoken as "the fraction a plus b divided by c", $\frac{a}{2}$ is spoken as "one half a". In addition, mathematical notation is inherently ambiguous, with the same notational construct being overloaded to mean different things in different contexts. Thus, the -1's in x^{-1} and $\sin^{-1} x$ have different meanings. The recognizer treats both occurrences of the -1 as a visual attribute of the object being superscripted. The decision to treat the -1 appearing as a superscript to the function as denoting the function inverse is made by rendering rules based on special patterns.

Since such interpretation is context sensitive, the quasi-prefix representation is enhanced —before an object is rendered, *special-pattern* (a memoized[7] function) is called to identify *special patterns.* A user can specify additional patterns by providing method definitions on function *special-pattern* for specific object types. These special patterns can then be turned on by calling

(*turn-on-special-pattern* <*object-name*>).

The user can provide rendering rules named <*pattern*> for object <*object*>, which get invoked when the particular special pattern is seen. Individual special patterns can be turned off by executing statement

[7] A memoized function remembers its results between invocations for efficiency.

(*turn-off-special-pattern* <*object-name*>).

All special patterns can be turned off by deactivating style *use-special-patterns.*

Special patterns built into AsTeR include:

- 2 as the superscript is interpreted as squaring, 3 as cubing etc.
- T as the superscript of a valid matrix expression denotes transpose.
- -1 as the superscript of a function name denotes function inverse.
- D_x^n denotes a derivative.

4.5 Descriptive Renderings

In Sec. 4.3, we described a succinct audio notation for mathematics. However, renderings that are more descriptive also sound more natural. As mentioned earlier, the extent to which we use descriptive renderings is an entirely subjective choice. This section presents some descriptive AFL rendering rules from AsTeR.

Rendering Integrals

The various parts of an integral have special meaning. Using the audio notation would produce a rendering that cues the subscript and superscript on the integral, leaving it to the listener to interpret their meaning. Rule *descriptive* for object *integral* (see Fig. 4.6) interprets the subscript and superscript as the limits of integration. Integrals having no superscript are interpreted as surface integrals. The rule also correctly identifies the variable of integration in the majority of examples.

We have a similar rendering rule for summations that interprets the subscript as a constraint on the summation. The rule also correctly renders examples where the subscript and superscript to the summation operator give the lower and upper bound on the range of summation.

Obtaining Different Views

We can think of rendering rules as producing a particular "display" of a given structured object. Thus, in a system like (LA)TEX, the author of a macro picks a specific layout for objects appearing in the document. This choice, once made, holds throughout the rendering of the document. On an interactive system like AsTeR, the listener can pick different ways of "hearing" the same object[8].

[8] The author has found this feature very useful in understanding difficult mathematical proofs.

```
(def-reading-rule (integral descriptive)
    "Descriptive rendering  rule for integrals"
     (let ((lower-limit (subscript integral ))
           (upper-limit (superscript integral ))
           (children (children integral))
           (pause-amount (compute-pause integral ))
           (var (variable-of-integration integral)))
       (afl:with-surrounding-pause pause-amount
            (read-aloud " Integral ")
            (cond
              ((and lower-limit upper-limit)
               (read-aloud "from  ")
               (when var (read-aloud (children var))
                     (read-aloud " equals" ))
               (read-aloud lower-limit)
               (afl:pause 1)
               (read-aloud " to ")
               (read-aloud upper-limit)
               (afl:pause 1))
              (lower-limit
               (when var (read-aloud " with respect to ")
                     (read-aloud (children var )))
               (read-aloud " over, ")
               (read-aloud lower-limit ))
              (var (read-aloud "with respect to ")
                   (read-aloud (children  var ))))
            (afl:force-speech)
            (read-aloud (first children)) (afl:force-speech)
            (read-aloud var) (afl:subclause-boundary))))
```

Fig. 4.6. Descriptive rendering rule for integrals.

In CS611, a course on advanced programming languages, we work with proof trees. Proof trees typically have a set of premises that lead to a conclusion. A typical rendering of a proof tree is:

We know that ...; Hence we infer ....

On the other hand, another rendering rule might "display" the same structure as:

We can conclude ... because we know ....

This has the effect of inverting a proof tree. We perform such actions all the time when perusing written material. On the other hand, when listening to recorded books on tape, a listener is tied down to the one rendering order that the reader chose to use. In contrast, AsTeR allows the listener to determine the rendering order by activating different rules, thus enabling better comprehension of complex material.

Here is another example from the same course. The following rules show different ways of rendering occurrences of operator *subst* (textual substitution). They allow the listener to "look" at a particular expression from different perspectives. $R[S/T]$ denotes R with T replaced by S. The linear "display" used to layout this expression on paper is just one possible linearization of operator *subst*. When speaking this expression, the description can be formulated in several ways.

$R[S/T]$ is written using macro `\subst`, a macro that takes three arguments. AsTeR is first extended to recognize this macro call into object *subst* having three *arguments* as follows:

```
(define-text-object :macro-name "subst" :number-args 3
  :processing-function subst-expand :object-name subst
  :precedence mathematical-function :supers (math))
```

Instances of `\subst` occurring in the document are now represented as instances of object *subst*. Object *subst* has its argument slot set to a list containing the result of processing the arguments to the `\subst` call. Function *argument* can be used to access these within rendering rules. Here are some AFL rules to generate different renderings of this object.

English descriptions The next two rendering rules use plain English to produce a descriptive rendering. They are good rules to use when the concept of substitution is being introduced. However, they do not work well for more complex examples like $R[X/Y][S/T]$.

```
(def-reading-rule (subst english-active)
    " english-active rendering  rule for object subst."
  (let  ((pause-amount (compute-pause subst)))
    (afl:with-surrounding-pause pause-amount
      (read-aloud (argument subst 1 ))
      (read-aloud " with ")
      (read-aloud (argument subst 2))
      (read-aloud " for  ")
```

```
      (read-aloud (argument subst 3 )))))

  (def-reading-rule (subst english-passive)
      " english-passive rendering  rule for object subst."
    (let((pause-amount (compute-pause subst)))
      (afl:with-surrounding-pause pause-amount
        (read-aloud (argument subst 1))
        (read-aloud " with ")
        (read-aloud (argument subst 3))
        (read-aloud "replaced by ")
        (read-aloud (argument subst 2 )))))
```

Linear rendering The following linear rendering rule mimics the visual notation. It is succinct, since it avoids words like "brackets", instead relying on voice changes to convey the nesting. It is a good alternative to the tree-like rendering.

```
  (def-reading-rule (subst linear)
      " linear rendering  rule for object subst"
    (read-aloud  (argument subst 1))
    (afl:new-block
     (afl:local-set-state (reading-state 'dim-children))
     (read-aloud  (argument subst 2))
     (read-aloud " slash " )
     (read-aloud (argument subst 3))))
```

Tree-like rendering The following produces a "tree-like" rendering of object *subst* by displaying it as a prefix ternary-operator. It is a good rule for rendering complex *subst* objects once the listener is familiar with the concept of textual substitution. It is very succinct and conveys nesting effectively.

```
  (def-reading-rule (subst tree-like)
      " tree-like rendering  rule for object subst."
    (read-aloud "substitution ")
    (afl:new-block
     (afl:local-set-state (reading-state 'dim-children))
     (read-aloud (argument subst 1))
     (read-aloud (argument subst 2))
     (read-aloud (argument subst 3))))
```

where

```
(reading-state 'dim-children)
```

generates a new AFL state along dimension *dim-children*; see Fig. 4.2.

4.6 Variable Substitution

The preceding sections have demonstrated the use of AFL in writing audio rendering rules for conveying complex structures. However, oral communication takes more time than written communication, and the listener has to retain a lot more information than a person perusing printed text. This disadvantage is most felt when listening to complex mathematics. It takes time to speak complicated expressions and sometimes the listener has forgotten the beginning of an expression by the time it has been fully rendered.

Conjecture 4.6.1. Top-level structure: An experienced reader of mathematical formulae first looks at the top-level structure of a complex equation, and then progressively reads the subexpressions.

Thus, given Faa De Bruno's formula:

$$D_x^n w = \sum_{0 \leq j \leq n} \sum_{\substack{k_1+k_2+\cdots+k_n=j \\ k_1+2k_2+\cdots+nk_n=n \\ k_1,k_2,\ldots,k_n \geq 0}} D_u^j w \frac{n!(D_x^1 u)^{k_1} \cdots (D_x^n u)^{k_n}}{k_1!(1!)^{k_1} \cdots k_n!(n!)^{k_n}} \tag{4.5}$$

We see it as an equation with a derivative on the LHS and a double summation on the RHS. We then see that the inner summation has a complicated constraint and that the summand is a fraction. Finally, we read the entire expression.

The steps enumerated above are carried out implicitly by the eye, making it difficult to identify the atomic actions involved. Yet, it is clear that we rely on this type of breaking up or "chunking" of complex expressions when understanding them. In fact, most of visual mathematical notation is an attempt at aiding this process of grouping subexpressions together in a meaningful manner —even in the visual setting, writing out Faa De Bruno's formula in a fully linearized manner (e.g., the TEX encoding) makes comprehension difficult, if not impossible.

In the audio setting, the listener does not have the luxury of being able to view both the top level structure as well as the leaves of the formula when listening to a straight rendering of the expression. This means that ASTER needs to take over part of the work that was described as being implicit in the visual context —ASTER needs to recognize and convey the same kind of grouping that the experienced reader perceives in the visual notation.

We call this process rendering with *variable substitution.* Thus, given a complex expression of the form $\frac{e_1}{e_2}$, where the e_i are complex math expressions, ASTER recognizes this top-level structure and produces the rendering, "Fraction x over y, where x is $\cdots$ and y is $\cdots$". In the following subsections, we enumerate the conditions under which such variable substitution is performed. Based on these, we have implemented a *variable substitution* rendering style. The listener can activate this style and have ASTER perform variable substitution where appropriate.

Examples

To motivate the discussion, here are some examples of how variable substitution can produce renderings that are easier to understand.

$$I = \int_0^\infty e^{-x^2}\, dx \tag{4.6}$$

would be spoken as

> i = integral with respect to x from 0 to infinity of f dx,
> where f is ...

This technique is particularly useful when presenting very complex equations. Variable substitution transforms 4.5 to:

$$D_x^n w = \sum_{0 \le j \le n} \underbrace{\sum_{\substack{k_1+k_2+\cdots+k_n=j \\ k_1+2k_2+\cdots+nk_n=n \\ k_1,k_2,\ldots,k_n \ge 0}}}_{\textit{lower constraint 1}} D_u^j w \frac{\overbrace{n!(D_x^1 u)^{k_1} \cdots (D_x^n u)^{k_n}}^{\textit{numerator 1}}}{\underbrace{k_1!(1!)^{k_1} \cdots k_n!(n!)^{k_n}}_{\textit{denominator 1}}} \tag{4.7}$$

which can now be rendered as:

> Enneth derivative with respect to x of w equals
> Summation over 0 less than or equal to j less than or equal to n
> Summation over *lower constraint 1* of
> jayth derivative of u with respect to x times the fraction
> *numerator 1* over *denominator 1*. where *lower constraint 1* is ...,
> *numerator 1* is ...,
> *denominator 1* is ....

It takes 68 seconds to speak 4.5, making it difficult to perceive the top-level structure from listening to a straight rendering of the expression. Using style *variable substitution*, the top-level expression is rendered in 23 seconds, and it takes a further 57 seconds to render the substitutions. Thus, though the total time taken to speak the entire expression is more, the listener can understand the top-level structure in about a third of the time it would take to listen to the entire expression.

Variable substitution should be used sparingly, since renderings using this style take a longer time to convey entire expressions, in this example, 80 seconds against 68 seconds—AsTeR uses variable substitution only if an expression is sufficiently complex.

Criterion for Applying Variable Substitution

The following enumerates a few of the points to be considered when designing a variable substitution scheme.

1. Minimize the number of levels of substitution. Ideally this should not be more than 1.

2. Avoid unnecessary substitutions. In 4.6, substituting a variable for the entire right-hand side is redundant.
3. Use a complexity measure that determines when an expression is sufficiently complex to warrant variable substitution. This measure should capture the following properties of an expression:
   a) Complexity of a math object considered by itself.
   b) Relative complexity of an expression with respect to its parent.

Motivation for above Criteria

The first requirement says that any variable substitution scheme we apply should result in a simple top-level expression. The second requirement ensures that the top-level expression conveys as much information as possible. In addition, it ensures that the renderings resulting from variable substitution do not end up being more complicated than plain renderings. Thus, in 4.6, substituting identifier x for the entire right-hand side to produce

> i equals x where x equals ...

does not simplify the rendering. This is because the top-level expression is a relation, and substituting for one of the sides of a relation only produces a new relation which is as complex as the original. The third requirement ensures that all expressions are compared using the same weighting scheme. Measure *weight* described in Sec. 4.4 is used.

We introduce the notion of *relative complexity* below:

Definition 4.6.1. *Relative Complexity:*
Given expression e with child c_i with weight(e) $= w$ and weight(c_i) $= w_i$,

$$\textit{relative-complexity}(c_i) = \frac{w_i}{w} \tag{4.8}$$

Basic Algorithm

Here is a sketch of the variable-substitution algorithm. It uses three user-specified complexity thresholds, whose purpose will become clear in the following description.

Given an expression e, compute its weight w. Do not perform substitutions if $w <$ **absolute-complexity-threshold**. Otherwise, e is a good candidate for variable substitution.

First try to substitute for the children of e. Given children c_i $\{1 \leq i \leq n\}$, compute their weights w_i. Substitute for a child c_i if and only if its relative complexity is greater than **proportional-complexity-threshold**. Thus, for each i, if $w_i \geq w\cdot$ **proportional-complexity-threshold**, apply the algorithm recursively to c_i. If no substitution can be performed on the descendants of c_i, replace c_i itself.

If no substitution can be performed on any of the c_i or their subexpressions, then substitute for e provided that e is not a top-level expression. Also do not substitute if e is one of the sides of a relational.

Given a top level expression e having weight w, this algorithm is called as follows:

```
(collect-substitutions e (complexity-threshold e))
```

where *(complexity-threshold e)* is defined as:

```
(defun complexity-threshold  (object)
  "Compute the threshold value for  this object"
  (let ((proportional
         (+ 1 (truncate
               (* (weight object )
                  *proportional-complexity-threshold* )))))
    (max proportional *absolute-complexity-threshold*)))
```

Instead of computing $\frac{w_i}{w}$ < **proportional-complexity-threshold**, we initialize the algorithm with the threshold $w \cdot$ **proportional-complexity-threshold**, since w remains constant throughout the algorithm.

Refining the Algorithm

We now introduce the following refinements to the algorithm:

- If the parent expression is a relation, then do not perform substitutions on the children themselves. Proper subexpressions of the children are still considered for substitution.
- Consider attributes as well as the children of an expression for substitution.
- Use a different weighting scheme for deciding when to substitute for attributes by introducing a third constant, **attribute-complexity-threshold**. This constant is used to scale **proportional-complexity-threshold** when considering attributes.

Substitution Threshold Values

The following values were arrived at experimentally:

$$\begin{aligned} \texttt{*absolute-complexity-threshold*} &= 5 \\ \texttt{*proportional-complexity-threshold*} &= 1/7 \\ \texttt{*attribute-complexity-threshold*} &= 2.5 \end{aligned}$$

Naming the Substitution

AsTeR chooses identifier names that convey some information about the object being replaced. This has two advantages:

- An identifier like "summand" when referring to the expression appearing as the summand in a summation conveys more information than the identifier x.
- When substitutions are spoken after rendering the top-level expression, the listener finds it easier to relate them to the top-level expression.

Names for the substituted expressions are chosen using the following information:

- Type information. The objects returned by the recognizer are all typed. So at the very least, we have type information for all objects, e.g., mathematical function, parenthesized expression, etc.
- Contextual information. The first child of a fraction is called its "numerator". The left-hand side of an implication is called the "premise" and its right-hand side the "conclusion". We have built in this information for standard mathematical objects and provided a flexible mechanism for the user to add or modify such information.
- Special patterns: The special patterns presented in Sec. 4.4 are also used in synthesizing meaningful names for the substitutions.

Thus, when substituting for the subscript to a summation operator, ASTER uses the name "lower constraint". Since more than one such "lower constraint" may be substituted in a general expression, such names are appended with an integer to make them unique. This is how the rendering shown earlier for Faa De Bruno's formula is produced.

Additional Examples

The following illustrate the effect of applying variable substitution.

$$\underbrace{e^{x+e^{x+e^{x}+e^{x}}}}_{\textit{first term 1}}(1+\underbrace{e^{x+e^{x}+e^{x}}}_{\textit{first term 2}}(1+\underbrace{e^{x+e^{x}}(1+e^{x})}_{\textit{product 1}}))$$

The above expression has been annotated with underbraces to indicate the variable substitution that is performed. Notice that applying variable substitution reveals the recursive nature of the expression. It is interesting to note that if we now run our algorithm on this annotated expression, the subexpressions marked by underbraces are chosen for substitution.

Implementation Issues

We had to resolve some interesting implementation issues in order to provide the functionality described above. All the previously active rendering rules and styles work in conjunction with the variable substitution rendering style. This means that the expressions resulting from variable substitution are rendered exactly as they would be if they occurred by themselves. To achieve this, AsTeR first applies variable substitution and then applies the currently active rendering rules to the result. This added level of complexity is completely transparent to a user of AsTeR, who can continue to add rendering rules and modify styles in the presence of variable substitution.

4.7 Floating Objects

The concept of objects that *float* to the end of a page or chapter is well-known in the context of typesetting. Footnotes float to the end of the page, while figures may float to the end of a chapter. AsTeR provides the same functionality with rendering rules that delay audio rendering. In this section, we describe rendering rules that enable footnotes to float (in general instances of any object type) to the end of different hierarchical units in the document model.

We achieve this by first implementing a mechanism for delayed evaluation in *Lisp*.

(delay-until <trigger> <action>)

delays the execution of action *<action>* until triggered by *<trigger>*. In a rendering rule that *floats* an object, *<action>* is a function object whose body specifies audio events to be executed. The delayed action is triggered by executing

(force-if <trigger>)

This *forces* all actions that are waiting for *<trigger>* in the order in which they were *delayed*. The delayed evaluation provided by this mechanism is of course more widely applicable.

Example of a Floating Rendering Rule

We now give an example of a rendering rule[9] that floats instances of object footnote to the end of the containing paragraph. This rule uses *delay-until*.

```
(def-reading-rule (footnote float)
   "Make footnotes float to the end of containing paragraph. "
 (delay-until 'paragraph
              #'(lambda()
                  (without-rule (footnote float)
                                (read-aloud footnote )))))
```

After rendering instances of object O, function *read-aloud* forces all delayed actions that are triggered by the *class-name* of O. Thus, to make footnotes float to the end of the containing paragraph, all the user need do is to activate the above rendering rule. A rule that floats all figures[10] to the end of a chapter is:

[9] This is a simplified rule. This rule also takes care of rendering the footnote marker before delaying the rendering of the footnote text.

[10] Figures are rendered by speaking the figure caption.

```
(def-reading-rule (figure float)
    "Make figures  float to the end of containing chapter. "
  (delay-until 'chapter
               #'(lambda()
                   (without-rule (figure float)
                                 (read-aloud figure)))))
```

where *Lisp* macro (*without-rule* (<*o*> <*r*>) <*b*>) executes statements <*b*> with rule <*r*> for object type <*o*> deactivated.

Using Floating Renderings

The ability to delay the renderings of objects provides several interesting applications. The first of these is rendering the text of footnotes at the end of a paragraph or section, rather than where the footnote marker occurs in the running text. Such a rule is useful when rendering documents having several footnotes.

Note that footnotes float to the end of the logical unit of text in which they occur, rather than to the end of a physical unit like a page. Page breaks are completely irrelevant in the context of audio formatted output, since they are merely a consequence of the constraints placed by the physical page.

The general ability to float any object in the document model is a more powerful feature than is present in standard typesetting systems, which typically allow only certain objects to be floated. In AsTeR, given object types O_1 and O_2 where instances of O_2 occur as sub-objects of instances of O_1, we can write a rendering rule that delays the rendering of all instances of O_2 until the enclosing instance of O_1 has been completely rendered. Thus, instances of O_2 float to the end of the enclosing instance of O_1.

5. Browsing Audio Documents

5.1 Introduction

When perusing printed text, a reader can quickly skip portions of the document, reading only those sections that are of interest. Typeset documents allow such structured browsing by using layout cues to present the underlying document structure; from here, the eye's ability to "randomly" access portions of the two-dimensional printed page appears to take over. The passive information in a printed document is accessed by an active reader capable of selectively perusing the text. Hence, visual documents themselves need not be interactive.

Things are different with audio. This passive-active relationship is reversed in traditional oral communication; the information flows past a passive listener who has little control on what is heard. The problem is particularly severe when presenting structured information (e.g., complex mathematics) —a listener is likely to lose interest by the time the relevant information is presented. Hence, we need to enable active listening, i.e., enable the listener to determine what is heard. Therefore, to be effective, audio documents need to be interactive.

The first step is to make audio documents interactive. Techniques for specifying and modifying how particular objects are rendered were described in Sec. 4.1. In addition, a browser for audio documents allows a user to interactively traverse the internal high-level representation described in Chap. 2 and listen to portions of interest. The browser provides basic tree-traversal commands. These can be composed to effectively browse the information structure.

The design of our browser is motivated by the conjecture that most of visual browsing actions are directed by the underlying structure present in the information. Thus, when we read a complex mathematical expression that involves a fraction, we can quickly look at the numerator while reading the denominator. This single action of looking up at the numerator can be decomposed into a series of atomic tree traversal movements with respect to the structure of the expression. In the visual context, these actions happen extremely fast, leading to a feeling that the eye can access relevant portions of the visual display almost randomly. However, this notion of randomness disappears when we consider that such visual browsing becomes difficult in a badly formatted document where the underlying structure is not so apparent. Similarly, even when presented with a well-formatted document, a person unfamiliar with the subject matter finds it impossible to perform the same kind of visual browsing. Visual browsing thus depends on familiarity with the underlying structure and a clear rendering of this structure. AsTeR parallels this functionality by building up a rich internal representation and providing a set of atomic actions to traverse this representation. The effectiveness with which a user can browse this representation is now a function of the user's familiarity with the structure in the subject matter being presented.

We present the browser as follows: Sec. 5.2 motivates the need for a browser by analyzing how visual browsing works. Based on this, we derive a corresponding model for audio browsing. We identify a set of atomic browsing actions that enable general browsing. Sec. 5.3 describes how a user can traverse the high-level representation of a document. This section introduces the concept of a *current selection* and describes how the user is unobtrusively cued to the nature of the current selection. Sec. 5.4 describes how the listener can execute actions after setting the current selection. These actions include listening to the current selection, rendering it relative to its parent, and listening to the rest of the document. Cross-references form an important component of technical documents and are described in Sec. 5.5. A particularly difficult problem faced when listening to mathematical texts on conventional talking books, or even when reading printed mathematical texts, is keeping track of equation numbers and understanding statements that refer to equations and theorems by their numbers in the running text. We describe a flexible mechanism that allows a listener to annotate cross-referenceable objects with meaningful labels that can be used to refer to such objects in later cross-references. This section also describes how places of interest in a document can be marked using a bookmark facility. App. A.5 documents the external interface to the browser. The browser, along with the ability to change rendering rules and styles, makes audio documents produced by AsTeR fully interactive.

5.2 How Does Browsing Work?

Communication through the Printed Medium

As a first step towards developing an effective audio analogue, let us examine communication through the printed page. The printed page is passive: it is a two-dimensional visual display with marks on it. The person reading the printed page can either scan the material linearly or browse through parts of the document. Visual layout (the way the marks appear on paper) enables such browsing. Thus, rather than laying all the text in a naïve manner on the page, we exploit concepts such as line and paragraph breaks to allow the reader to perceive *chunks* of the printed matter and to selectively read specific portions of the text being presented.

The dpower of the printed medium lies in the eye's ability to browse text laid out on a two-dimensional display. When reading a paper, we are able to skim through the text, focusing on paragraphs of interest, and quickly scan across to the bottom of a page when we see a reference being made to a footnote.

The Audio Setting

The previous paragraph adopted the metaphor of a document being marks on paper. In contrast, in the audio setting, we have the ear, which is passive, and a document that is scrolling away in a linear fashion. This makes the goal of achieving an audio analogue to the printed page seemingly difficult.

An Alternative Model

The eye is certainly capable of moving to any point on the page extremely rapidly. Yet, when we browse, we do not move about randomly around the printed page. Typically, we move to the next paragraph, next line, or previous word. This seems to indicate that the eye infers some structure in the printed document, which is used to move around effectively. Since each of these actions are being performed extremely rapidly, owing to the eye's inherent scanning ability, these atomic actions are difficult to pinpoint.

We therefore conjecture the following: *Every well-formatted document presents inherent logical structure, which the eye is capable of perceiving. All visual browsing actions can be characterized as movements around this structure.*

A Naïve Example

Consider a well-formatted document containing no mathematical formulae. Here, the layout structure consists of a root node, which is the page, and the paragraphs which are the various children. At the next level on this tree, we have the lines, and each line is further broken up into words and words themselves are broken up into characters. Given this structure, we can rephrase all of the browsing actions as a combination of simple tree traversal movements. Thus, we can identify the following atomic actions:

1. Go to next sibling.
2. Go to previous sibling.
3. Go to parent.
4. Go to left most child.
5. Go to rightmost child.
6. Mark current node.

7. Return to marked node.

Using the above atomic actions and their various combinations, we can define all the browsing actions that the eye is capable of performing.

Thus, on encountering a reference to a footnote while reading we:

1. Mark current node.
2. Go to parent (this gets us out of the current paragraph).
3. Move across siblings until footnote is located.
4. Read footnote.
5. Return to marked node.

A Complex Example

Consider the following expression as read by a person familiar with mathematical notation:

$$\int \frac{e^{-x^2} + e^{x^3}}{\sin x^2 + \cos^2 x}\, dx$$

The experienced reader is able to quickly scan the above expression and, while perusing the denominator, access the numerator. This ability is a consequence of internalizing the underlying structure conveyed by the visual layout and using it to traverse the information. The atomic actions in accessing the numerator are:

1. Mark current node.
2. Read previous sibling.
3. Return to marked node.

We enable audio browsing by allowing a listener to perform the same kind of traversals. AsTeR internalizes a sufficiently rich structure to permit all of these browsing actions.

5.3 Traversing High-Level Document Structure

Our internal representation for document structure is an attributed tree. Tree structures are easy to traverse, and they provide a uniform way of browsing structure present in both plain text as well as mathematical formulae. This section outlines our approach to enabling such browsing actions.

All browsing actions are defined with respect to the *current selection* (a node in the internal tree representation of the document) that is recorded in variable **read-pointer**. Typically, the current selection is initially the top of the document. The current selection can be changed in two ways:

– Interrupting the current rendering by executing command *stop*[1] (bound to **s**). Commands *stop* and *quit* are described in detail in Sec. 5.4.

---

[1] Contrast this with command *quit* (bound to **q**).

- By moving the selection when no rendering is in progress. Typically, single key-strokes[2] execute the commands listed in the following paragraphs.

The following browser actions can be executed when no rendering is in progress. Our key-mapping for these commands is inspired principally by the key-map used by the *UNIX VI* editor.

- **t** Move to the top of the document.
- **C-u t** move to the top of the current math expression.
- **h**: Move left: set current selection to previous sibling.
- **l**: Move right: set current selection to next sibling.
- **j**: Move down: set current selection to first child.
- **k**: Move up: set current selection to parent.

Below, these browser actions are augmented to enable the traversal of the attributed tree structure defined in Chap. 2. In our model, all nodes have *content.*

- **i**: Move to content: set current selection to the contents of the current selection.

The following actions move the selection to the various attributes. The parent of an attribute is defined to be the object being attributed. The result of moving to attributes can therefore be undone by moving back up to the parent.

- ^: Move to superscript.
- _: Move to subscript.
- *: Move to accent.
- #: Move to underbar.
- !: Move to left subscript.
- %: Move to left superscript.

The above key-map[3] for traversing the attributes was arrived at as follows: The choice for superscript and subscript is automatic, since the keystrokes match the symbols used by TEX to markup these attributes. Placing the fingers on the row of numerals on a standard keyboard, the actions necessary for typing ^ and _ are mimicked with the left hand to arrive at the key-bindings for the left superscript and subscript. The middle finger of each hand is used to get to the accent/underbar.

Tables are the only objects in our internal representation that do not conform completely to the tree-traversal model. This is because each table element is linked to its parent as well as to its four neighbors. The left and

[2] The browser interface is implemented using Emacs Lisp. Key-strokes execute *EMACS* commands, which in turn send the right forms to the *Lisp* system. The browser interface will have to be re-implemented if the *Lisp* process is not being run inside *EMACS*.

[3] A user of ASTER is free to re-map these actions to other keys.

right neighbors can be modeled as siblings, but we need extra links and hence extra actions to traverse the entries by columns.

- **a**: Move to element above.
- **d**: Move to element below.

Summarizing the Selection

When any of the above browsing actions are executed, the new selection is summarized. These summaries are designed to be concise but informative. A typical problem that results when traversing complex structure is the so-called "lost in space" problem, where a user gets disoriented with respect to the current selection. We avoid this problem by conveying the following bits of information after each move:

- **Context**: Contextual information about where the current selection occurs with respect to the rest of the document.
- **Type**: The type of the current selection. Typically, this involves summarizing the current selection, which is described below.

Thus, when moving down the right hand side of Faa de Bruno's formula shown in 4.5, the listener would hear:

Key-press	Action	Context	Type
		Right hand side is	Summation
j	First child	Summand is	Summation
j	First child	Summand is	Juxtaposition
j	First child	First term is	Derivative
l	Next sibling	Second term is	Fraction
j	First child	Numerator is	Product
l	Next sibling	Denominator is	Product

Messages like the ones shown above have been found to be sufficient to avoid the lost-in-space problem mentioned earlier.

The nature of an object is conveyed by generic function *summarize* — methods on this function specify how individual object types are summarized. Below, we show some examples —the following list is not meant to be exhaustive. In cases where insufficient information is available to generate a complete summary of an object instance, the type of that object is spoken.

Object Type	Summary
Article	Title
Sectional unit	Section title
Complex Math object	Operator appearing at the root
Math object (leaf node)	Render node

Contextual information (e.g., what the children of math objects are called) is available to AsTeR, —children of an inference are called "premise" and "conclusion"; children of a fraction are called numerator and denominator. Such information was used to advantage in generating meaningful names when applying variable substitution; it is now exploited in giving contextual information about the current selection.

Traversing the structure of mathematical expressions is particularly useful when used in conjunction with the variable-substitution rendering style. In fact, such traversal can be thought of as a dual to variable substitution. If an expression has been rendered once using variable substitution, then future traversals of that expression use the variable names generated in the substitution process when cueing the current selection. This proves to be a very useful memory aid when understanding complex equations like Faa de Bruno's formula shown in 4.5.

Traversing document structure is also very useful when handling large documents, e.g., entire textbooks. The browser actions described so far enable the listener to move quickly through the document without having to listen to a lot of text. In conjunction with the ability to switch rendering styles, this enables the quick location of portions of interest. For instance, a listener can activate a rule (see Fig. 4.1) that renders only the mathematics in a document. Once an equation of interest is encountered, the listener can interrupt the rendering, move the current selection from this point to the enclosing paragraph or sectional unit, and then listen to the relevant portion of the document.

5.4 Rendering the Current Selection

The current selection is rendered by executing browser command *read-current*. The rendering commenced by *read-current* can be interrupted in two ways:

- *Quit*: Interrupt the current rendering and restore the current selection.
- *Stop*: Stop the rendering and leave the current selection at the object last rendered. Thus, executing *read-current* and *stop* moves the current selection.

Another browser action is to render the rest of the document starting from the current selection. This is enabled by browser command *read-rest* (bound to **c**).

Moving the selection to the next or previous node and then rendering is a common sequence of actions. AsTeR provides commands *read-previous* and *read-next* (bound to **p** and **n** respectively) that combine these actions.

In addition, the browser provides command *read-just-this-node* (bound to **r**) that renders only the current node, rather than the entire subtree rooted at this node —this is useful when traversing complex mathematical expressions.

Relative Renderings

In the above paragraphs, we described the various browser actions that render the current selection. The current selection can be rendered either as if it occurs by itself or as it would be if it were rendered along with the rest of the document. The former is straightforward; we need only execute generic function *read-aloud* on the current selection. The latter presents an interesting problem.

Specifying that the current selection should be rendered relative to its position in the entire document is analogous to picking a word from the electronic encoding of a book and asking the question:

> On what page in the book does this word appear?

In general, answering such a question would involve completely rendering the book. Analogously, rendering the current selection relative to its position in the document can be computationally intensive. We avoid this complexity by recording a pointer to the AFL state that is current when a document object is rendered. On the surface, this seems like it would require a lot of storage. In reality, this approach is both feasible and efficient, because the same AFL states are used to render a large number of the objects appearing in a document.

Recording of AFL states used to render specific objects is made possible by adding an extra slot named *afl-state* to object *document.* Initially, the value of this slot is *nil*, but when an object is rendered for the first time, a pointer to the AFL state that is current when the rendering commences is recorded in this slot. Relative renderings are produced by function *read-current-relatively* shown below. Notice the use of the AFL block in setting up a lexical scope for the duration of the rendering. Locally setting the AFL state to that recorded in slot *afl-state* of the object being rendered is sufficient to achieve the desired relative rendering.

```
(defun read-current-relatively()
  "Render current selection relatively"
  (save-pointer-excursion
   (cond
     ((afl-state *read-pointer*)
      (afl:new-block                         ;retrieve state
       (afl:local-set-state (afl-state *read-pointer*))
       (read-aloud *read-pointer* ) (afl:force-speech )))
     (t  (read-current )))))
```

Relative renderings are most useful when listening to tables and matrices. As described in the chapter on rendering rules (see Sec. 4.2), these are rendered using stereo effects, with the spatial location of the sound indicating the position of elements in the table. When moving through the elements of a table, hearing each element at the right spatial coordinate is useful in keeping track of the location of the current selection. Thus, the user can move the current selection to the rightmost column and then move down this column, hearing each element spoken on the right speaker. As another example of using relative renderings, consider traversing the right-hand side of Faa de Bruno's formula shown in 4.5. Moving to the subscript of the summation with _ and then executing *read-current-relatively* results in the constraint being rendered in the "subscript voice" —this cues the location of the current selection.

5.5 Cross-References and Bookmarks

This section describes how the browser allows the traversal of additional links introduced by cross-references in the document. Command *read-follow-cross-ref* (bound to **g**) is executed after interrupting the rendering. By default, this renders the next cross-reference in the document; a prefix argument[4] results in the previous cross reference being rendered. This is necessary — typically, the rendering will have been stopped close to, rather than, on a cross-reference. AsTeR also allows cross-reference links to be traversed while rendering is in progress. When a cross-reference is spoken, AsTeR plays a short sound cue that acts as a prompt. If the user responds with **y**, the cross-reference is rendered before continuing. The presence of this functionality almost obviates the need for the user to call command *read-follow-cross-ref* interactively.

How a cross-reference is rendered depends on the object being cross-referenced. For instance, rendering a cross-reference to a section results in the section number and title being spoken. This is more useful than just speaking the section number. Typically, the renderings of cross-reference tags are designed to give as much information as possible without being unduly verbose. Renderings of cross-reference tags are customizable by providing methods on generic function *read-cross-reference.* One such method is shown below.

```
(defmethod read-cross-reference ((section section))
  "Render a cross reference to a sectional unit."
  (read-aloud (section-name section ))
  (when (section-number section)
    (afl:speak-number-string (section-number section )))
  (afl:comma-intonation) (read-aloud (title  section ))
  (afl:comma-intonation) (afl:force-speech))
```

Cross-Referenceable Objects

Technical documents use cross-references to numbered equations and theorems to make the presentation succinct. Cross-references in the running text typically use a system-generated number, e.g., equation 3.2.1. Even when reading printed material, this convention can present problems. Consider, for instance, a proof that reads:

[4] Emacs terminology for C-u as a prefix to the command.

> By equation 3.1 and theorem 4.2 and equation 8, we get equation 9 and hence the result.

If the above is difficult to understand when reading it in print, it is unusable when encountered in a spoken document, where the listener does not have the luxury of quickly scanning back to the cross-references.

The ability to follow a cross-reference tag during the rendering does mitigate this problem to some extent. However, following such cross-references can prove distracting. AsTeR overcomes this by allowing the listener to label cross-referenceable objects with meaningful labels when they are rendered. These user-supplied labels are used when rendering cross-reference tags, almost eliminating the need to follow cross-references.

To give a concrete example, consider listening to a book on Fermat's last theorem. The first chapter might introduce the subject by stating the theorem. Assume that this theorem is numbered 1.1. The rest of the book might refer to this theorem by number, as in:

> As a corollary of this result, we can prove theorem 1.1.

When the corresponding document is rendered by AsTeR, the listener hears the theorem, the system generated number (theorem 1.1), and a fleeting sound cue. At this point, the user can give the theorem a more meaningful name by pressing **y** and entering an appropriate name. Assume the listener enters "Fermat's last theorem". Later, when rendering cross-references to this theorem, the newly entered label will be used instead of the system generated theorem number. Thus, the example shown above would be rendered as:

> As a corollary of this result, we can prove Fermat's last theorem.

Bookmarks

The browser also provides a simple bookmark facility, which can be used to mark positions of interest to be returned to later. Browser command *mark-read-pointer* (bound to **m**) prompts the user for a bookmark name and marks the current position. Command *follow-bookmark* (bound to **f**) takes a bookmark name and returns to the marked position. Bookmarks can be accessed in two ways: **f** renders the marked object without moving the current selection and **C-u f** resets the current selection to the marked position.

6. Related Work

This chapter presents a review of the published literature relevant to our work. In producing audio renderings, we draw on prior work on structured electronic documents and the use of speech and non-speech audio in computer interfaces.

Sec. 6.1 introduces work on recognizing document structure. We outline ongoing work on marking up document structure unambiguously and translating between different document encodings. Sec. 6.2 covers prior and ongoing work in the innovative use of audio in human-computer interaction.

6.1 Electronic Documents

Electronic document systems are based on:

1. Markup-based approaches.
2. Layout-based approaches.

Marking Up Document Structure

Standard Generalized Markup Language (SGML) marks up document logical structure in a layout-independent manner [SGM86, Org90, HPR92, Gol90]. A Document Type Definition (DTD) is used to encapsulate the logical structure of specific classes of documents. Thus, SGML provides a notation for describing classes of structured documents and for coding documents belonging to described classes. An advantage of SGML and other grammar-based document representations is the ability to perform multiple applications on a single document source file. The International Committee on Accessible Documents (ICAD) has been working on defining an accessible DTD[1], but at present their work does not encompass mathematical content.

Though SGML is now used to markup a variety of documents by many government agencies, it still has very little support for marking up technical content, e.g., mathematics. There is ongoing work to remedy this situation. In

[1] See Sec. B for some frequently asked questions about accessible documents and our answers.

the last year, the SGML-Math committee has been working on a math DTD for SGML. This work is not yet complete, but it has raised a few interesting issues. The main point of discussion has been whether it is possible to design a math DTD that captures semantic information about the mathematical constructs being marked up. Though it would be nice to have all of a mathematical construct's semantic content when processing the document, e.g., in our case producing audio renderings, this seems almost unattainable. There is as yet no firm agreement on this point, but the trend seems to be to move towards a math DTD that captures the layout as embodied by TEX. Defining a DTD that captures full mathematical semantics would make it difficult to invent new notation. TEX, by only capturing the layout constructs used to build up written mathematics, side-steps this issue, and the resulting system makes it easy to invent new notation. However, this also makes recognition more difficult. Some of the problems present in (LA)TEX are being addressed by ongoing work on the LATEX3 project.

Significant work has been carried out in the context of structure-sensitive editors for documents. This work has focused on the design of appropriate document encodings that capture high-level structure unambiguously. Another topic of interest has been the capture of hypertext links within the context of structured documents. The logical structure of documents is typically captured using a tree-like representation consisting of hierarchical units. The challenge of integrating this model with the notion of hypertext links has been successfully addressed by the design of HyperText Markup Language (HTML), an SGML-based markup system for encoding structured hypertext documents. Finally, the aim of achieving the best of two worlds, i.e., the power afforded by a grammar-based markup system and the user-interface provided by WYSIWYG systems (what you see is what you get) has led to work on providing multiple synchronized views of a document [Har88]. See [QV92, LG90, BB90, KLMN90, PI88, SF88, SF90, FBN+90, Lev88, SFR92, FS89, Kat87, Ass86, KS84, CJ90, BG90, Ver90, PS88, QNA90, Bro88] for details on relevant work in this area.

Translating between Different Markup Languages

There has been some work towards building automatic translators for converting electronic documents from one markup language to another. The need for such systems is apparent: Even though most of today's documents get written electronically, it is still practically impossible to exchange electronic documents generated on disparate computer systems. This means that the only way information can be exchanged is by first printing a hardcopy.

There are two approaches to solving this problem:

1. Recognize high-level structure in the form of abstract syntax and then convert the abstract syntax representation to any desired concrete syntax.
2. Produce an output form that is the least common denominator of the various high-level representations and then exchange this version.

Producing abstract syntax. ICA (Integrated Chamelion Architecture), was developed at the Computer Science Department in Ohio State University [MOB90]. The system produces translators between different document encodings. Users specify an abstract syntax for the class of documents they wish to translate. Typically, this abstract syntax would be similar to a DTD used by SGML. Users then specify the conversion rules for mapping this abstract syntax to and from the concrete syntax used by different markup systems. Using this specification, the system generates translators that can convert documents from a specific concrete syntax to the abstract syntax and vice-versa.

The advantage of this approach is that it requires only $O(n)$ translators to convert between documents encoded in n different markup languages. Directly translating between the n markup systems would require $O(n^2)$ translators. The difficulty is that not all markup systems use the same model for the same class of documents. This means that the abstract syntax can capture only those features that are common to all n markup systems. To give an example, one of the target systems might explicitly capture section numbers in the markup, while the other might compute them upon request.

Converting to the least common denominator. Given documents marked up in n different markup languages, an alternative solution is to convert all of them to a form that is the least common denominator of the various document encodings. This can be done by converting the documents either to plain ASCII or to a display-specific format, such as Postscript. Both these alternatives have shortcomings as outlined below.

Converting to ASCII loses layout structure. Since the only thing that cues logical structure in a formatted document is layout, this form of conversion loses information.

An alternative solution is adopted by systems like the Adobe Acrobat. Page Description Format (PDF), a portable form of Postscript, is used by the Adobe Acrobat as a common currency between different computing platforms. The encoded document can be displayed with its original layout on disparate computing platforms without using the software used to produce the original document. This solution does allow users to exchange documents without losing any layout information. However, it is only one step better than exchanging printed paper: exchanging PDF files is like exchanging electronic paper! For example, the information present in the document cannot be manipulated electronically. This also means that the information and its inherent structure can be accessed in only one way —by a human looking at the information. The principal advantage of having information online —the ability to process it— is lost. In addition, it has the serious disadvantage of making electronic information inaccessible to persons with special needs.

Recognizing Document Logical Structure

Most recognition work has focused on extracting logical structure from document layout. Significant research has been carried out in the context of OCR-based document recognition. For a complete bibliography on work in this area, we refer the reader to the online bibliography on document understanding available on the Internet[2].

See [PR92] for details on recognizing logical structure from the layout information present in a Postscript file. This is a difficult problem and re-emphasizes the earlier comment on PDF and the shortcomings in storing electronic documents in a purely layout-oriented form.

Relatively little work has been done in recognizing document structure from electronic markup. The work on Chamelion [MOB90] and related work in the area of attribute grammars [Yel88] could be used to extract logical structure from electronic documents. Tools such as the Cornell Synthesizer Generator [RT84, RT88a, RT88b] and the Centaur system [Bor88] can also be used to build such recognizers. The key to building such recognizers successfully is the robustness and applicability of the high-level models used. For details on other attempts at recognizing structure from markup, see [Arn91, AM91, AW91, Arn92].

Mathematical Notation

One of our principal aims when designing AsTeR was to produce clear and succinct audio renderings for mathematics. In designing a concise audio notation for mathematics, it is interesting to note that the written mathematical notation that we have come to accept is relatively new. For an in-depth survey of the evolution of written mathematics, see [Caj30].

There is little similarity between developing a written notation and its audio counterpart. However, the evolution of written notation shows the following. Any notational system is a combination of conventions and an intuitive use of the various dimensions that are provided by the perceptual modality and the means available to produce output appropriate for that modality. In the case of visual notation, these dimensions are font size, changes in baseline, use of different delimiters, stacking of sub-expressions to build up layout, and the use of characters from different scripts. This insight enabled us to develop a concise audio notation for spoken mathematics that exploits the various audio dimensions that are currently available —see Sec. 4.3 for details. It is conceivable that the number of audio dimensions will increase with the improvement in audio hardware, leading to a more sophisticated audio notation.

---

[2] *URL* FTP://dimund.umd.edu/pub/DOCBIB/databases/DocumentBib.bib

6.2 Summary of Work in Audio Interfaces

This section presents a brief executive summary of the various research projects that are related to incorporating audio as an additional dimension to computer interfaces.

Speech Synthesis

There are three approaches to producing digitized speech:

1. Concatenative: Concatenate digitized utterances produced by a human to make up canned messages.
2. Diphone: Use a library of diphones obtained by sampling a large number of utterances spoken by a human.
3. Formant: Model the human vocal tract by using a series of cascading filters to produce the right wave forms and hence intelligible speech.

Approach 1 is space intensive. It works in a limited number of cases, but it has the advantage of producing the most natural sounding speech in a restricted domain.

Approach 2 is more widely applicable and provides an unlimited vocabulary. It is memory intensive, since the diphones (numbering about 3, 000 for English) need to be accessed frequently. The approach is not compute intensive. Quality varies widely from barely intelligible to human-intelligible. This approach has been commercially applied by Apple in the form of MacinTalk-1 and MacinTalk-2. The MacinTalk-2, also known as GalaTea, is fairly memory intensive, but the quality is among the best that has been achieved with this method of synthesis. The principal drawback with diphone synthesis is that the underlying model is fairly restrictive. Though systems like GalaTea achieve a fair amount of intonation, the intonational structure generated still leaves much to be desired. The model also allows only minimal variations in voice, e.g., pitch and speech rate. Changing voice parameters produces a significant deterioration in output.

Approach 3, which models the human vocal tract, is compute but not memory intensive. It is also the most flexible approach to speech synthesis. Since it is based on a mathematical model of the human vocal-tract, it permits a large number of variations in voice quality (see [Kla87, Her89, Her90, Her91] for details). What is more, it allows us to perform the same kind of scaling etc. on the voice that we perform in the visual setting when working with fonts. This is particularly useful in conveying complex information and is exploited in our own work in presenting spoken mathematics.

Audio as a Data-Type

The practical problem of how audio data should be managed has been addressed in order to deal with the following issues:

- Real-time compression of audio data.
- Changing speech rate in digitized audio without modifying pitch. This is referred to as time-scale modification [RW85].
- Producing spatially located sounds (directional audio).
- Conversion between various encoding schemes.
- Exchanging audio data between disparate hardware.
- Broadcasting audio data over networks for teleconferencing. Significant work has been done in the context of the Internet m-bone, the multicast backbone.
- Client/server solutions to allow user applications to transparently access audio resources.

The work done at DEC CRL on the *AudioFile* [LPT+93] project is particularly significant in using audio resources effectively. *AudioFile*, using the same conceptual model as the X-windows system, provides a client/server model for accessing audio devices on a variety of platforms. Several applications such as answering machines can be very easily built on top of *AudioFile*, which is publicly available from *FTP://crl.dec.com/pub/DEC/AF*. The speech skimmer project at the MIT Media Labs allows a listener to interactively skim recorded speech and listen to it at several levels of detail. See [Aro93b, Aro92b, Aro92a, SASH93, Aro91b, Aro93a, SA89, ABLS89, ASea88, Aro91a, Aro92c] for work carried out in the Speech Group at the MIT Media Labs on manipulating digitized speech and audio.

CSOUND, a music synthesis system developed at MIT by Barry Vercoe, can be used for real-time synthesis of complex audio. Researchers at NASA Ames have developed the convolvotron [WF90, WWK91], a system for real-time synthesis of directional audio. The convolvotron is computationally intensive, but the power available on today's desktop has seen the development of scaled-down versions of this technology in the form of QSOUND for the Apple and Intel-486 platforms.

Non-Speech Audio in User Interfaces

Non-speech audio can be used in innovative ways to augment conventional output devices such as a visual display. Today, most desktop computers can produce at least telephone-quality audio. Non-speech audio has been used for a long time on the Apple platform to provide the user with audio cues for specific events. This work has been formalized by the human-computer interaction community by introducing the notion of earcons [SMG90, JSBG86, BCK+93, BGP93, Ram89, RK92, BG93, Gav93, BGB88, Bux89]. A screen access program (prototype) for Presentation Manager under OS2 demonstrated the effective use of such non-speech cues in providing the user with spatial information —see [F.92] for details. A similar approach is being used at Georgia Tech in developing Mercator[3] [ME92], a

[3] See *FTP://cc.gatech.edu/multimedia/papers/Mercator* for online papers.

screen access program for the X-windows system. The use of non-speech audio to display complex data sets has been investigated by the scientific visualization community, where audio provides an extra dimension (see [BGK92, BLJ86, Ram89, RK92, Bro92, Bro91, SB92] for several related examples).

Information Presentation in Audio

Work in speech synthesis and linguistics has considered the problem of presenting information using speech. The question of achieving the right intonational structure is addressed by [Gro86, DH88, Pie81, HP86, HW84, HLPW87, PH90, HW91, Hir91, Hir90a, Hir90b, WH91]. See [LOS76, Str78, OKDA73, ZP86] for an analysis of the intonational cues used by human speakers when speaking mathematical expressions. A set of guidelines for presenting spoken mathematics is outlined in [Cha83] and has been used by the Recordings for the Blind (RFB) in producing mathematical texts in talking book format.

Presenting information orally can be applied in several situations. [Dav89] describes a system for providing oral instructions to an automobile driver. Refer to [DT87, Dav88, DS89, DS90] for related work on this project.

Information Browsing

With the advent of remote access systems to information databases, the need for effective browsing techniques has received attention in several research projects. Notable among these is Paul Resnick's PhD work [Res92] at MIT. His thesis proposes a flexible model for quick and effective information browsing by modeling the information structure as a series of linked lists.

Structure-based browsing has been in vogue in the hypertext community for several years. Many results from this area are directly relevant to information browsing in audio. Notable among these is the work in defining Hypertext Markup Language (HTML), a hypertext analogue to SGML. The World-Wide Web (WWW), an HTML-based hypertext information retrieval system is widely used on the Internet. WWW browsers allow a user to quickly access a wide variety of information sources. The Webb currently contains textual as well as audio and video resources. At present, only primitive browsing of audio/video data is possible, since there is very little structure available in digitized audio/video data.

Browsing Digitized Audio/Video Data

Relatively little research has been carried out in this area so far. The potential presented by the availability of a large volume of digitized audio/video data was first outlined in [LB87]. The need to browse such data efficiently will prove essential if we are to survive the age of the 1,000 television channels!

Approaches used so far are characterized by the use of word spotting to identify context from the digitized audio data and using such contextual information to access portions of interest from the audio/video data stream. On the global Internet, the availability of Internet Talk Radio and other sources of large audio data provide an excellent research test-bed.

A. Documentation

This chapter documents the different modules of AsTeR. The entire system is about 33,000 lines of *LISP-CLOS* code, and documenting each function here would make this appendix prohibitively long. Therefore, only those commands that will be used by a general user are documented.

A.1 Setting Up AsTeR

This section details the hardware and software configuration necessary for running AsTeR —detailed installation instructions can be found with the source code.

Hardware Requirements

AsTeR currently uses a MultiVoice synthesizer [Tec91], a serial-line text-to-speech device based on the Dectalk 3.0. The MultiVoice provides independent software control on the volume of the speaker and headphone ports. Since this is currently missing from the Dectalk, AsTeR cannot produce directional speech if a Dectalk is used.

AsTeR is implemented under Lucid Common Lisp/SPARC 4.0.2. AsTeR relies heavily on *CLOS* support and is presently running on a SPARC IPC with 24MB of memory. The Common Lisp process communicates with the MultiVoice connected to either of the serial ports, `/DEV/TTYA` or `/DEV/TTYB`. It is currently assumed that the Common Lisp process is run on the local workstation.

Software Environment

AsTeR has an *Emacs* front-end. Common Lisp is run as a sub-process of *Emacs* (version 18.59.1 or 19), using the *Emacs ILISP* interface.

Once the source code has been installed, AsTeR can be started up from within *Emacs* by executing *M-x aster*. This starts up a Common Lisp sub-process and loads in all of the code, compiling it if necessary. At this time, the voice synthesizer should be connected and powered on, since AsTeR communicates with the device when starting up to make sure that all is well. The user hears spoken messages as each module of AsTeR is successfully loaded.

A.2 The Recognizer

This section documents the external interface to the recognizer.

parse-article *filename* [*FUNCTION*]

> Recognize document contained in file *filename* and construct a high-level representation, which is returned as a document object. Assumes that the document in file *filename* is a valid (LA)TEX document.

do-not-signal-error-on-unknown-tex-macro *t* [*VARIABLE*]

> If *nil*, the recognizer signals a continuable error upon encountering a new user-defined TEX macro in the document being recognized. Default is not to signal an error.

define-text-object &key *macro-name number-args processor precedence arguments object-name supers* [*MACRO*]

> Extend the recognizer to handle instances of a newly defined TEX macro. The keyword arguments are:

Description	Type	Keyword
TEX macro name	string	*macro-name*
Number of arguments	number	*number-args*
Name to use	symbol	*processor*
Represented as	symbol	*object-name*
Super-classes	list	*supers*
Contextual names	list	*arguments*

define-new-environment &key *env-name object-name* [*MACRO*]

> Extend the recognizer to handle user-defined environments in LATEX. *env-name*, a string, is the name of the new environment. *object-name*, a symbol, is the name of the object that represents instances of this environment.

define-math-classification *string classification* [*FUNCTION*]

> Classify token *string* as of type *classification*. This is how tokens are classified for processing in math mode.

define-precedence *operator* &key *same-as* [*FUNCTION*]

> Define precedence for operator *operator* to be the same as existing operator *same-as*.

show-precedence-table [*FUNCTION*]

> Show one entry from each row of precedence table. Entries are listed in ascending order of precedence.

A.3 AFL

This section documents the *LISP-CLOS* functions and macros that make up AFL. Note that symbols like new-block that provide the external interface to AFL are exported symbols of package AFL; hence, all names are written without the package prefix, afl:.

The following are common to all the components of AFL.

new-block &body *body* [*MACRO*]

> AFL block statement. Introduce a local instance of variable *current-speech-state*; set it to the instance of *current-speech-state* that was referenceable just before execution of the block; and execute *body* within this local scope. Within the block, all (free) occurrences of *current-speech-state* refer to the new local variable. Upon termination of the block, destroy local variable *current-speech-state* and reset the state of the underlying hardware to its pre-existing state. The AFL block also functions as a cobegin statement. A block terminates only after all events commenced within it have finished executing.

terminate-block [*FUNCTION*]

> The currently-executing AFL block is terminated immediately. A browser can execute this statement when the audio rendering of an object is to be prematurely terminated because of a user interrupt.

local-set-state *new-state* [*GENERIC FUNCTION*]

> Set AFL local state to *new-state*. The type of *new-state* determines which component is set. Each component subspace provides a method on this function to perform the necessary actions when its state is set.

global-set-state *new-state* [*GENERIC FUNCTION*]

> Set AFL global state to *new-state*. The type of *new-state* determines which component is set. Each component subspace provides a method on this function to perform the necessary actions when its state is set.

The following subsections document the different component subspaces of AFL. Each component subspace provides methods on the generic functions corresponding to the AFL assignment statements. For the sake of brevity, we will not document each of the individual methods.

A.3.1 The Total Audio Space

The total audio space is the cross product of the component subspaces. Its state variable is an n-tuple made up of the state variables of the component subspaces.

initialize-total-space [*FUNCTION*]

Create and initialize AFL variables that encapsulate the local and global state of the total audio space.

current-total-audio-state *nil* [*VARIABLE*]

AFL total state in the current local scope.

global-total-audio-state *nil* [*VARIABLE*]

AFL total state in the global scope.

A.3.2 The Speech Component

Initializing the speech space.

initialize-speech-space &optional *(voice *default-voice*)* [*FUNCTION*]

Initialize speech space by setting up local and global speech state. Optional argument *voice* is the name of a point in speech space to which these should be initialized —the default is **default-voice**.

default-voice *'paul* [*VARIABLE*]

Name of default voice used to initialize speech space.

global-speech-state *nil* [*VARIABLE*]

Contains global speech state of AFL.

current-speech-state *nil* [*VARIABLE*]

Contains local speech state of AFL.

re-initialize-speech-space &optional *(voice *default-voice*)* [*FUNCTION*]

reinitialize speech space with *voice*, the name of a point in speech space.

Speech space operators. The speech space operators do not cause any side-effects.

move-by *(point point-in-speech-space) dimension offset* &key *(slot 'value)* [*METHOD*]

Return point reached by moving from *point* along *dimension* by *offset*. Default is to change the dimension value. If called with *:slot 'step-size*, modify the step size instead.

step-by *(point point-in-speech-space) dimension n-steps* &key *(slot 'value)* [*METHOD*]

Return point reached by moving from *point* by *n-steps* along *dimension*. Default is to change the dimension value. If called with *:slot 'step-size*, modify the step size instead.

move-to *(point point-in-speech-space) dimension-value* &key *(slot 'value)* [*METHOD*]

Return point reached by moving from *point* along *dimension* to *value*. If called with *:slot 'step-size*, modify the step size instead.

scale-by *(point point-in-speech-space) dimension scale*&key *(slot 'value)* [*METHOD*]

Return point reached by scaling value along *dimension* by *scale*. If called with *:slot 'step-size*, modify the step size instead.

multi-move-by *(point point-in-speech-space)* &rest *settings* [*METHOD*]

Move from *point* along several dimensions; *settings* is a list of dimension-value pairs.

multi-move-to *(point point-in-speech-space)* &rest *settings* [*METHOD*]

Move from *point* along multiple dimensions; *settings* is a list of dimension-value pairs.

multi-scale-by *(point point-in-speech-space)* &rest *settings* [*METHOD*]

Return the result of scaling *point* along multiple dimensions, where *settings* is a list of dimension-value pairs.

multi-step-by *(point point-in-speech-space)* &rest *settings* [*METHOD*]

Return result of stepping along multiple dimensions from *point*, where *settings* is a list of dimension value pairs.

generalized-afl-operator *(point point-in-speech-space)* &rest *settings* [*METHOD*]

Operate on *point* and return result. *Settings* is a list of triples — operation, dimension, value.

set-final-scale-factor *dimension factor* [*FUNCTION*]

Set final scale factor for *dimension* to *factor*. Final scaling is applied before producing output.

Speech events.

pause *milliseconds* [*FUNCTION*]

Insert *milliseconds* milli-seconds of pause.

send-text *text* [*FUNCTION*]

Send *text* to the speech device.

speak-number *number-string* [*FUNCTION*]

Send *number-string* to the speech device.

force-speech [*FUNCTION*]

Force speech immediately. Used when speech is to be produced before a sentence end marker has been sent.

with-surrounding-pause *pause-amount* &body *body* [*MACRO*]

Execute *body* with surrounding pause specified by *pause-amount*.

Intonational structure.

comma-intonation [*FUNCTION*]

Generate a comma intonation. Applies to the clause last sent.

period-intonation [*FUNCTION*]

Generate a period intonation. Applies to the clause last sent.

interrogative [*FUNCTION*]

Send an interrogative intonation. Applies to the clause last sent.

exclamation [*FUNCTION*]

Send exclamation intonation. Applies to the clause last sent.

exclamatory-stress [*FUNCTION*]

Send exclamatory stress. Applies to the next phrase to be sent.

primary-stress [*FUNCTION*]

Send primary stress. Applies to the next phrase to be sent.

secondary-stress [*FUNCTION*]

Send secondary stress. Applies to the next phrase to be sent.

subclause-boundary [*FUNCTION*]

Insert a subclause boundary. Applies to the next phrase to be sent.

high-intonation [*FUNCTION*]

Generate H*, rising intonation. Applies to the next phrase to be sent.

low-intonation [*FUNCTION*]

Generate L*, falling intonation. Applies to the next phrase to be sent.

high-low-intonation [*FUNCTION*]

Generate Hl, rise and fall intonation. Applies to the next phrase to be sent.

paragraph-begin [*FUNCTION*]

Begin a paragraph, rising pitch. Applies to the next phrase to be sent.

Points in speech space.

save-point-in-speech-space *name point* [*FUNCTION*]

Associate *name* with *point*, a point in speech space.

define-standard-voice *name* &rest *settings* [*FUNCTION*]

Define a standard voice named *name* specified by *settings*, a list of dimension-value pairs.

get-point-in-speech-space *name* [*FUNCTION*]

return predefined point named *name*.

Dimensions in speech space.

list-of-speech-dimensions [*FUNCTION*]

Return list of speech-space dimension names.

minimum-value *dimension* [*FUNCTION*]

Return minimum value for *dimension*.

maximum-value *dimension* [*FUNCTION*]

Return maximum value for *dimension*.

dimension-range *dimension-name* [*FUNCTION*]

Return difference between maximum and minimum values for dimension *dimension*.

length-of-subinterval *dim n* [*FUNCTION*]

Return length of a subinterval when dimension *dim* is subdivided into $n - 1$ subintervals.

A.3.3 The Non-Speech Audio Component

Initializing the non-speech component.

initialize-audio-space [*FUNCTION*]

Create and initialize the local and global states of the non-speech component to default values.

global-audio-state *nil* [*VARIABLE*]

Contains global state of the non-speech audio component.

current-audio-state *nil* [*VARIABLE*]

Contains local state of the non-speech audio component.

The non-speech audio space provides methods on the generic functions for the assignment statements.

Non-speech space operators.

select-sound *(point point-in-audio-space) (sound string)* [*METHOD*]

Return point with this *sound* selected. *Sound* is the name of a sound-file.

select-sound *(sound string) (point point-in-audio-space)* [*METHOD*]

Return point with this *sound* selected. *Sound* is the name of a sound file.

switch-on *(point point-in-audio-space)* &key *(synchronize nil)* [*METHOD*]

Return a new point with its switch turned on. Executes asynchronously by default. Call with *:synchronize t* to synchronize with other ongoing events.

switch-off *(point point-in-audio-space)* &key *(synchronize nil)* [*METHOD*]

Return a new point with its switch turned off. Executes asynchronously by default. Call with *:synchronize t* to synchronize with other ongoing events.

toggle-switch *(point point-in-audio-space)* &key *(synchronize nil)* [*METHOD*]

Return point, with its audio-player switched toggled.
Executes asynchronously by default. Call with *:synchronize t* to synchronize with other ongoing events.

play-once *(point point-in-audio-space)* [*METHOD*]

Play the sound selected by *point* once.

move-to *(point point-in-audio-space) dimension value* &key &allow-other-keys [*METHOD*]

Move from *point* to *value* along *dimension*.

Non-speech events.

synchronize-and-play *soundfile* &key *(background-flag nil)* [*FUNCTION*]

wait until all ongoing simple events have stopped executing and then play *soundfile*, an audio file. If *background-flag* is *t*, then the sound is played in the background (asynchronously).

Pronunciation

define-pronunciation *string pronounced-as* &key *(mode :text)* [*FUNCTION*]

Define *pronounced-as* as the pronunciation for string *string*. The default is to define this pronunciation for *text* mode. In general, *mode* is a keyword symbol that names a pronunciation mode.

A.4 Rendering Information Structure

This section documents the commands associated with defining rendering rules, changing rendering styles, and the post-processing required to generate context sensitive renderings.

A.4.1 Processing the Quasi-Prefix Form

weight *object* [*GENERIC FUNCTION*]

Compute the weight of object *object*. weight is a complexity measure used to compare mathematical objects. Weight is a memoized function: it remembers its results between calls.

balanced-tree-p *(math-object math-object)* [*METHOD*]

Return *t* if tree rooted here is balanced, i.e., all the children have the same weight.

special-pattern *object* [*GENERIC FUNCTION*]

Define the special patterns that should be looked for when processing *object*. Methods on this function for specific object types specify such patterns in the form of a case statement, with one case for each pattern to be identified. Rendering rules that should be applied when special patterns are seen, can be defined. Example: If we specify *'half* as the special pattern for $\frac{1}{2}$, then we can define a rendering rule named *'half* for object *math-object*. Activating style *use-special-patterns* and executing turn-on-special-pattern with argument *math-object* results in the newly defined rule being used when rendering expressions containing $\frac{1}{2}$. This function is memoized: it remembers its results between computations.

A.4.2 Rendering Rules and Styles

read-aloud *object* [*GENERIC FUNCTION*]

Render object *object* in audio. An around method on this function for the principal object type, document, calls the currently active rule for *object*. Primary methods on read-aloud for *object* serve as default rendering rules. Rendering rules should use read-aloud, rather than a specific rule, to render sub-objects —unless a specific rendering is to be hard-wired into the rule.

current-reading-style [*FUNCTION*]

Return names of currently active rendering styles.

activate-style *style* [*FUNCTION*]

Activate style *style*.

deactivate-style *style* [*FUNCTION*]

Deactivate style *style*.

activate-rule *object-name rule-name* [*FUNCTION*]

Activate rule *rule-name* for object *object-name*.

deactivate-rule *object-name* [*FUNCTION*]

Deactivate currently active rule for object *object-name*.

reading-rule *object-name rule-name* [*GENERIC FUNCTION*]

Methods on this generic function define named rendering rules. *object-name* is the name of a document object type. *rule-name* is a symbol that names the rule. Rendering rules are methods on this generic function that specialize on both object type and rule name. Users of ASTER should use the interface provided by Lisp macro def-reading-rule when defining new rules.

def-reading-rule *(object-name rule-name)* &body *body* [*MACRO*]

This macro provides a transparent interface to the underlying implementation of rendering rules. *object-name* names the object type, *rule-name* is the name of the rendering rule, and *body* is the body of the rendering rule. This macro expands to the appropriate method on generic function *reading-rule*.

rem-reading-rule *object-name rule-name* [*MACRO*]

Remove rendering rule *rule-name* for object *object-name*. This macro provides an easy-to-use interface to the *CLOS* function remove-method.

trace-reading-rule *object-name rule-name* [*MACRO*]

Trace rendering rule *rule-name* for object *object-name*. This macro provides an easy-to-use interface to the *CLOS* function remove-method.

doc-reading-rule *object-name rule-name* [*MACRO*]

Return documentation for rendering rule named *rule-name* for object type *object-name*.

turn-on-special-pattern *object-name* [*FUNCTION*]

Turn on special patterns for object type *object-name*. If special patterns are turned on, a known special pattern is seen and rendering style *use-special-patterns* is active then ASTER uses a rule that is appropriate for this context.

turn-off-special-pattern *object-name* [*FUNCTION*]

Turn off special patterns for object *object-name*.

A.5 The Browser

This section documents the browser. Below, *current position* refers to the current position in the document being browsed. The object at this current position is referred to as the *current selection*. The phrases "moving current position" and "changing current selection" are used synonymously.

Current Position

read-pointer [*FUNCTION*]

Return current position in the document. This points to the object that was just rendered.

save-pointer-excursion &body *body* [*MACRO*]

Preserve the current position in the document when rendering the current selection. This macro remembers the current position in the document and restores it afterexecution of *body*. Note: Current position is accessible by calling read-pointer.

Moving in the Browser

move-up &optional *(n 1)* [*FUNCTION*]

Move current position *up* by n levels. The defaultthe is one level.

move-forward &optional *(n 1)* [*FUNCTION*]

Move current position forward (to the right) by n. The default is to move to the next sibling.

move-back &optional *(n 1)* [*FUNCTION*]

Move current position backward (to the left) by n. The default is to move to the previous sibling.

move-above [*FUNCTION*]

If in a table, then move to the element above the current selection. Produce an appropriate spoken message if on the top row of a table.

move-below [*FUNCTION*]

If in a table, then move to the element below the current selection. Produce an appropriate spoken message if on the bottom row of a table.

move-to-children [*FUNCTION*]

Move to the children of the current selection.

move-to-contents [*FUNCTION*]

Move to the contents of the current selection.

move-to-top-of-math [*FUNCTION*]

Move to the top of the current mathematical expression —the root of the internal tree representation.

The next six functions move the current position to the various attributes of a math object.

move-to-subscript [*FUNCTION*]

Move to subscript.

move-to-superscript [*FUNCTION*]

Move to superscript.

move-to-accent [*FUNCTION*]

Move to accent.

move-to-underbar [*FUNCTION*]

Move to underbar.

move-to-left-superscript [*FUNCTION*]

Move to left-superscript.

move-to-left-subscript [*FUNCTION*]

Move to left-subscript.

forward-sentence &optional *(c 1)* [*FUNCTION*]

Move forward c sentences. Move back if c is negative.

Summarize

summarize *document* [*GENERIC FUNCTION*]

Summarize a document object. Methods on this function specify how different object types are summarized. Summarizing an object produces a succinct audio rendering sufficient to cue the listener to the identity of the object.

Rendering in the Browser

read-current *[FUNCTION]*

Render the object at the current position, indicated by read-pointer. Object will be rendered in the global state.

read-current-relatively *[FUNCTION]*

Same as read-current except that the object is rendered in the context in which it occurs. Especially useful when browsing table entries; using this function places them at the correct spatial location.

Calling any of the following functions affects current position.

read-previous &optional *(n 1)* *[FUNCTION]*

Render left sibling if any. *n* specifies amount by which to move left.

read-next &optional *(n 1)* *[FUNCTION]*

Render right sibling if any. *n* specifies amount by which to move right.

read-children *[FUNCTION]*

Render the children of the object at the current position.

read-parent &optional *(n 1)* *[FUNCTION]*

Move *up* by *n* levels and render the resultant selection. The default is to move up one level and render the parent.

read-rest *start-position* &optional *(read-this-node t)* *[FUNCTION]*

Render rest of the document starting at the current position. Optional argument *read-this-node* specifies if current selection should be rendered as well.

read-above *[FUNCTION]*

If in a table, then render the element above the element at the current position. Produces appropriate spoken message if on the top row of a table or outside a table.

read-below *[FUNCTION]*

If in a table, then render the element below the element at the current position. Produces appropriate spoken message if on the bottom row of a table or outside a table.

read-just-the-node *[FUNCTION]*

Render only the node at the current position. Useful when browsing mathematical expressions. Use this function to listen to the current term rather than the entire sub-expression rooted at current position.

read-sentence &optional *(count 1)* [*FUNCTION*]

REnder the next *count* sentences.

Cross References

follow-cross-ref-wait *1* [*PARAMETER*]

The value of this parameter determines how cross-reference tags are rendered. If *follow-cross-ref-wait* = 0, then the cross-reference tag is rendered and the system continues without waiting to check if the user wishes to follow the cross-reference. If *follow-cross-ref-wait* = n, then ASTER prompts the user by playing *cross-ref-cue* (a short sound cue) and waits for n seconds before continuing. If the user presses "y" in this time, the cross-referenced object is rendered.

read-follow-cross-ref *direction-flag* [*FUNCTION*]

Follow and render the closest cross reference.

Bookmarks

mark-read-pointer [*FUNCTION*]

Mark current location of read pointer.

remove-bookmark *tag* [*FUNCTION*]

Remove this bookmark.

follow-bookmark [*FUNCTION*]

Prompt for a bookmark and render the object marked by it. Does not affect the current position in the document.

goto-bookmark [*FUNCTION*]

Prompt for bookmark and move to this position. Affects current position in the document.

A.6 Some CLOS Terminology

This section defines some basic *CLOS* terminology. We refer the reader to [Ste90, X3J93] for additional details. The definitions given in this section are derived from an online copy of a draft standard for *CLOS*, Common Lisp Object System Specification, by Daniel G. Bobrow, Linda G. DeMichiel, Richard P. Gabriel, Sonya E. Keene, Gregor Kiczales, and David A. Moon.

CLOS Concepts

CLOS is an object-oriented extension to Common Lisp as defined in *Common Lisp: The Language*, by Guy L. Steele Jr. It is based on generic functions, multiple inheritance, declarative method combination, and a meta-object protocol.

The fundamental objects of *CLOS* are *classes*, *instances*, *generic functions*, and *methods*.

A *class* object determines the structure and behavior of a set of other objects, which are called its *instances*. Every Common Lisp object is an *instance* of a class. The class of an object determines the set of operations that can be performed on the object.

A *generic function* is a function whose behavior depends on the classes or identities of the arguments supplied to it. A generic-function object contains a set of methods, a parameter list (lambda-list), a method combination type, and other information. The *methods* define the class-specific behavior and operations of the generic function; a method is said to *specialize* a generic function. When invoked, a generic function executes a subset of its methods based on the classes of its arguments.

A generic function can be used in the same ways that an ordinary function can be used in Common Lisp; in particular, a generic function can be used as an argument to **funcall** and **apply**.

A *method* is an object that contains a method function, a sequence of *parameter specializers* that specify when the given method is applicable, and a sequence of *qualifiers* that is used by the *method combination* facility to distinguish among methods. Each required formal parameter of each method has an associated parameter specializer, and the method will be invoked only on arguments that satisfy its parameter specializers.

Using CLOS

A class can inherit structure and behavior from other classes. A class whose definition refers to other classes for the purpose of inheriting from them is said to be a *subclass* of each of those classes. The classes that are designated for purposes of inheritance are said to be *superclasses* of the inheriting class.

A class C_1 is a *direct superclass* of a class C_2 if C_2 explicitly designates C_1 as a superclass in its definition. In this case, C_2 is a *direct subclass* of C_1. C_n is a *superclass* of C_1 if there is a series of classes $C_2, \ldots, C_{n-1}$ such that C_{i+1} is a direct superclass of C_i for $1 \leq i < n$. In this case, C_1 is a *subclass* of C_n.

A class can inherit slots (named fields) and methods from its superclasses. A subclass inherits methods in the sense that any method applicable to all instances of a class is also applicable to all instances of any subclass of that class. The set of names of all slots accessible in an instance of a class C is the union of the sets of names of slots defined by C and its superclasses.

Like an ordinary Lisp function, a generic function takes arguments, performs a series of operations, and perhaps returns useful values. An ordinary function has a single body of code that is always executed when the function is called. A generic function has a set of bodies of code, of which a subset is selected for execution. The selected bodies of code, called the effective method, and the manner of their combination are determined by the classes or identities of one or more of the arguments to the generic function and by its method combination type.

In standard method combination, primary methods are unqualified methods and auxiliary methods are methods with a single qualifier that is one of **:around**, **:before**, or **:after**. *Primary methods* define the main action of the effective method, while *auxiliary methods* modify that action in one of three ways.

1. **:before** Method specifies code to be executed before applicable primary methods. Applicable **before** methods are executed in most-specific-first order.
2. **:after** Method specifies code to be executed after all applicable primary methods. **After** methods are executed in most-specific-last order.
3. **:around** Method specifies code to be run instead of applicable primary methods. The most specific **around** method is called first, and it can pass control to other **around** methods and, when no other **around** method is applicable, to the most-specific primary method.

The method combination facility controls the selection of methods, the order in which they are run, and the values that are returned by the generic function. *CLOS* offers a default method combination type, called standard method combination, and provides a facility for declaring new types of method combination.

An online *CLOS* tutorial by Jeff Dalton, *E-mail*: ⟨`J.Dalton@ed.ac.uk`⟩, is available at *URL* FTP://aiai.ed.ac.uk/lisp/random/.

B. Accessibility

This chapter defines what we mean by accessible documents and attempts to dispel some common misconceptions. Throughout this appendix, we address the question of accessibility of electronic information as it affects persons with visual impairments.

Access To Computers

A common mode of providing access to computers has been to design screen-reading programs, which allow a user to read different parts of a computer display using text-to-speech. Such screen-reading programs are currently used to provide access to electronic information as well. Typically, the information is displayed on the visual display, and the screen-reading application is used to listen to the text. This approach does provide access to plain textual information. However, it breaks down when presenting technical information, e.g., written mathematics, tables, and other forms of highly structured information.

This break-down is a consequence of visually formatted information presenting the underlying structure using purely layout-oriented cues. When a screen-reading program speaks such visually laid out information, the underlying structure is not conveyed. To give an example, consider a table of numbers. When this is spoken by a screen-reading program (a line at a time), it is impossible to perceive the underlying structure.

In general, this kind of break-down happens constantly when structured information is spoken by a screen-reading program. When we read visual documents, we perform structured browsing. In general, this is impossible when using the traditional paradigm of displaying information visually and reading aloud this display.

Note that though the previous paragraphs are critical of the approach taken by traditional screen-reading programs, they should be regarded not as a criticism of the screen-reading paradigm itself. Screen-readers are designed to give access to computer applications and are appropriate[1] for the tasks

[1] This thesis was written using IBM Screen Reader, a screen-reading program, to provide access to the visual display.

for which they were originally designed. What we point out here is that it is incorrect to overload the screen-reading programs with tasks for which they were not designed. There is a distinct shift in paradigms between providing access to a visual display and presenting structured information orally, and it is this shift in paradigm that we emphasize.

How structured information is presented orally should not be constrained by the way it is displayed visually. Visual information is laid out in a manner most suited to the visual mode of interaction; oral information should be presented in a manner most suited to oral communication.

Accessible Document Encodings

Using the screen-reading paradigm to provide access to electronic information has resulted in a common misconception that an accessible document is an ASCII document. This is not true! Though a large number of ASCII documents (electronic documents that contain plain text with no control codes) are accessible using screen-reading software, ASCII documents that use implicit visual layout in the form of spacing and vertical alignment are inaccessible. Thus, an ASCII display of a fraction or table is inaccessible for the reasons pointed out in the previous section.

This thesis has focused on the issue of presenting structured information orally with a view to conveying the underlying structure using audio layout. This kind of oral presentation requires full access to both the information as well as its underlying structure. Based on our experience, we define accessibility of a document encoding as follows:

1. Amount of structural information captured by the encoding.
2. The extent to which this structural information is available for processing by other applications.
3. The availability of the appropriate software needed to process this structure.

Thus, document encodings such as Postscript and PDF[2] are inaccessible because extracting document structure from purely visual layout is hard. Similarly, the internal format used by WYSIWYG (What you see is What you get) systems is inaccessible, since the assumed mode of presentation is visual.

Document encodings using markup languages such as (LA)TEX are better suited for oral access to information, because they encode the information in a layout independent manner. As pointed out in the chapter on recognition (see Chap. 2), extracting high-level structure from the (LA)TEX source, though possible, is fairly involved.

[2] PDF (Page Description Format) is a portable form of exchanging visually formatted information used by the Adobe Acrobat.

The advantage of grammar-based systems like (LA)TEX is that they encapsulate the information in a manner that allows alternative processing. This advantage is fully realized by Standard Generalized Markup Language (SGML), which provides the best possible choice for accessible encodings. Note, however, that a document does not become accessible simply by being encoded in SGML. The accessibility of an SGML document is determined by the Document Type Definition (DTD) to which it adheres. Thus, a DTD that does not capture any high-level structure leads to inaccessible SGML documents.

Online Books

The author has used ASTER to read the following books. The electronic sources were made available to him by their authors and publishers. These books proved invaluable as online references and also allowed us to test ASTER on a sufficiently large collection of documents.

Table B.1. Online books read using ASTER.

Text	Author
Lisp	Patrick Winston and Bertold Horn
Structure and Interpretation of Computer Programs	Harold Abelson and Gerald Sussman
Paradigms of AI Programming	Peter Norvig
LATEX A Document Preparation System	Leslie Lamport
The Design and Analysis of Algorithms	Dexter C. Kozen
Matrix Computations	Charles Van Loan and Gene Golub
Computational Framework for the Fast Fourier Transform	Charles Van Loan
Algebraic Computation	Richard Zippel
Mathematica: A Practical Reference	Nancy Blachman
A Logical Approach to Discrete Mathematics	David Gries and Fred Schneider
Nonlinear Optimization: Computational Issues	Steve Vavasis
Topics in Commutative Ring Theory	Irving Kaplansky
Ouvres Mathematiques d'Evarist Galois	English translation
Introduction to C Programming	Brian Kernighan and and Dennis Ritchie
AWK	Brian Kernighan
A C++ Primer	Stanley B. Lippman
CS611 Programming Languages	Lecture notes
CS681 Design and Analysis of Algorithms	Dexter Kozen Lecture Notes
Bulletins of the AMS	(American Mathematical Society)

The works by Kaplansky and Galois were made available by Prof. Keith Dennis of the Mathematics department.

References

[ABLS89] B. Arons, C. Binding, K. Lantz, and Christopher Schmandt. A voice and audio server for multimedia workstations. *In Proceedings of Speech Tech*, pages 86–89, May 1989.

[AM91] Dennis S. Arnon and S. Mamrak. On the logical structure of mathematical notation. *Proceedings of the TEX Users Group*, 12:479–484, July 1991.

[Arn91] Dennis Arnon. *DocTypes: A Methodology for Managing Structured Documents of Multiple Types.* Xerox PARC, April 1991.

[Arn92] Dennis S. Arnon. Model-directed conversions of LATEX documents. *Proceedings of the TEX Users Group*, July 1992. To be published.

[Aro91a] B. Arons. The design of audio servers and toolkits for supporting speech in the user interface. *Journal of the American Voice I/O Society*, pages 27–41, March 1991.

[Aro91b] B. Arons. Hyperspeech: Navigating in speech-only hypermedia. *In Hypertext '91 ACM*, pages 133–146, 1991.

[Aro92a] B. Arons. A review of the cocktail party effect. *Journal of the American Voice I/O Society*, pages 35–50, July 1992.

[Aro92b] B. Arons. Techniques, perception, and applications of time-compressed speech. *In Proceedings of 1992 American Voice I/O Society*, pages 169–177, September 1992.

[Aro92c] B. Arons. Tools for building asynchronous servers to support speech and audio applications. *UIST '92. Proceedings of the ACM Symposium on User Interface Software and Technology*, pages 71–78, November 1992.

[Aro93a] B. Arons. Hyperspeech. *ACM SIGGRAPH Video Review, InterCHI 93 Technical Video Program*, 1993. videotape.

[Aro93b] B. Arons. Interactively skimming recorded speech. *Proceedings of the User Interfaces Sofware and Technology (UIST) conference, ACM*, November 1993.

[ASea88] B. Arons, Christopher Schmandt, and et al. The VOX audio server, version 1.0. *Olivetti Research Center*, August 1988.

[Ass86] Association of American Publishers. *Markup of Mathematical Formulas*, April 1986. Electronic Manuscript Series.

[AW91] Dennis S. Arnon and Carl Waldspurger. *Meddle: A Structure Editor for Mathematical Notation*, February 1991. Draft Manuscript.

[BB90] Jr. Allen L. Brown and Howard A. Blair. A logic grammar foundation for document representation and document layout. In *Proceedings of the International Conference on Electronic Publishing, Document Manipulation & Typography*, pages 47–64. Cambridge University Press, September 1990.

[BCK+93] Robin Bargar, Meera M. Blattner (Chair), Gregory Kramer, Julius Smith, and Elizabeth Wenzel. Panel: Effective uses of nonspeech audio in virtual reality. *Proceedings of the IEEE Symposium on Research Frontiers in Virtual Reality*, October 1993.

[BG90] Eric A. Bier and Aaron Goodisman. Documents as user interfaces. In *Proceedings of the International Conference on Electronic Publishing, Document Manipulation & Typography*, pages 249–262. Cambridge University Press, September 1990.

[BG93] M. M. Blattner and R. M. Greenberg. *Communicating and learning through non-speech audio. Multimedia Interface Design in Education.* NATO ASI Series. Springer-Verlag, February 1993.

[BGB88] W. Buxton, W. Gaver, and S. Bly. The use of nonspeech audio at the interface. *Tutorial Notes, CHI '88.*, 1988.

[BGK92] M. M. Blattner, . M. Greenberg, and M. Kamegai. Listening to turbulence: An example of scientific audiolization. *Multimedia Interface Design*, pages 87–102, 1992.

[BGP93] Meera M. Blattner, Ephraim P. Glinert, and Albert L. Papp. *Sonic Enhancements for 2-D Graphic Displays, and Auditory Displays.* To be published by Addison-Wesley in the Santa Fe Institute Series. IEEE, 1993.

[BLJ86] M. M. Blattner, Mansur D. L., and K. I. Joy. Sound-graphs: A numerical data analysis method for the blind. *Proceedings of the Hawaiian International Conference on System Science*, 1986.

[Bor88] P. Borras. Centaur: the system. In *Proceedings of the SIGSOFT'88, Third Annual Symposium on Software Development Environments*, Boston, Massachusetts, 1988.

[Bro88] Kenneth P. Brooks. A two-view document editor with user-definable document structure. *DEC SRC Research Report*, 1(33), November 1988.

[Bro91] Mark H. Brown. Color and sound in algorithm animation. Technical report, DEC Systems Research Center, 130 Lytton Avenue, Palo Alto, CA 94301, August 1991.

[Bro92] Mark H. Brown. Zeus: A system for algorithm animation and multi-view editing. Technical report, DEC Systems Research Center, 130 Lytton Avenue, Palo Alto, CA 94301, February 1992.

[Bux89] W. Buxton. Introduction to this special issue on nonspeech audio. *Human Computer Interaction*, 4(1):1–9, 1989.

[Caj30] Florian Cajori. *A History of Mathematical Notations*, volume I-II. The Open Court Publishing Company, Chicago, IL., 1928-1930. Contents: vol. I. Notations in elementary mathematics. vol. II. Notations mainly in higher mathematics.

[Cha83] Larry A. Chang. *Handbook for Spoken Mathematics.* Lawrence Livermore National Laboratory, 1983.

[CJ90] Gil C. Cruz and Thomas H. Judd. The role of a descriptive markup language in the creation of interactive multimedia documents for customized electronic delivery. In *Proceedings of the International Conference on Electronic Publishing, Document Manipulation & Typography*, pages 277–290. Cambridge University Press, September 1990.

[Dav88] James R. Davis. A voice interface to a direction giving program. Technical Report 2, MIT Media Laboratory Speech Group, April 1988.

[Dav89] James R. Davis. *Back Seat Driver: Voice Assisted Automobile Navigation.* PhD thesis, Massachusetts Institute of Technology, September 1989.

[DH88] James R. Davis and Julia Hirschberg. Assigning intonational features in synthesized spoken directions. In *Proceedings of the Association for Computational Linguistics*, pages 187–193, 1988.

[DS89] James R. Davis and Christopher Schmandt. The back seat driver: Real time spoken driving instructions. In *Vehicle Navigation and Information Systems*, pages 146–150, 1989.

[DS90] James R. Davis and Christopher Schmandt. Discourse strategies for conversations in time. In *Proceedings of the AVIOS 1990 Conference*, pages 21–26, 1990.

[DT87] James R. Davis and Thomas F. Trobaugh. Direction assistance. Technical Report 1, MIT Media Laboratory Speech Group, December 1987.

[F.92] Jr. McKiel F. Audio-enabled graphical user interface for the blind or visually impaired. *Proceedings of the Johns Hopkins National Search for Computing Applications to Assist Persons with Disabilities (Cat. No.92TH0429-1)*, pages 185–7, 1992.

[FBN+90] Richard Furuta, Heather Brown, Steven R. Newcomb, Roberto Minio, Vincent Quint, Roy Rada, and Laurence A. Welsch. Hypertext and electronic publishing. In *Proceedings of the ECHT'90 European Conference on Hypertext*, Panels, pages 347–353. Cambridge University Press, 1990.

[FS89] Richard Furuta and P. David Stotts. Programmable browsing semantics in trellis. In *ACM Hypertext'89 Proceedings*, Navigation in Context, pages 27–42. ACM, 1989.

[Gav93] William Gaver. Synthesizing auditory icons. *Proceedings of INTERCHI 1993*, pages 228–235, April 1993.

[Gib96] Wayte Gibbs. Envisioning speech. *Scientific American*, September 1996.

[Gol90] Charles F. Goldfarb. *The SGML handbook.* Oxford: Clarendon Press; Oxford; New York: Oxford University Press, 1990.

[Gro86] Barbara J. Grosz. Attention, intentions, and the structure of discourse. *Computational Linguistics*, 12(3):175–204, July–September 1986.

[Har88] Michael Harrison. *Vortex: An interactive document preparation system*, volume 236 of *Lecture Notes in Computer Science*, page 21. Springer Verlag, January 1988.

[Hay96] Brian Hayes. Speaking of mathematics. *American Scientist*, 84(2), March–April 1996.

[Her89] Susan R. Hertz. The delta programming language: An integrated approach to non-linear phonology, phonetics and speech synthesis. *Papers in laboratory phonology I: Between the grammar and the physics of speech*, 1989.

[Her90] Susan R. Hertz. A modular approach to multi-dialect and multi-language speech synthesis using the delta system. *Proceedings of the workshop on speech synthesis*, 1990.

[Her91] Susan R. Hertz. Streams, phones and transitions: Towards a new phonological and phonetic model of formant timing. *Journal of Phonetics*, 19:91–109, 1991.

[Hir90a] Julia Hirschberg. Assigning pitch accent in synthetic speech: The given/new distinction and deaccentability. In *Proceedings of the Seventh National Conference*, pages 952–957, Boston, 1990. American Association for Artificial Intelligence.

[Hir90b] Julia Hirschberg. Using discourse context to guide pitch accent decisions in synthetic speech. In *Proceedings of the European Speech Communication Association Workshop on Speech Synthesis*, pages 181–184, Autrans, France, 1990.

[Hir91] J. Hirschberg. Using text analysis to predict intonational boundaries. In *Proceedings of the Second European Conference on Speech Communication and Technology*, Genoa, 1991. ESCA.

[HLPW87] J. Hirschberg, D. Litman, J. Pierrehumbert, and G. Ward. Intonation and the intentional structure of discourse. In *Proceedings of IJCAI-87*, Milan, 1987. International Joint Conference on Artificial Intelligence.

[HP86] J. Hirschberg and J. Pierrehumbert. The intonational structuring of discourse. In *Proceedings of the 24th Annual Meeting*, pages 136–144, New York, 1986. Association for Computational Linguistics.

[HPR92] E. Van Herwijnen, N. A. F. M. Poppelier, and C. A. Rowley. Standard DTDs and scientific publishing. *EPSIG News*, 3:10–19, 1992.

[HW84] J. Hirschberg and G. Ward. A semantico-pragmatic analysis of fall-rise intonation. In *Proceedings of the 20th Meeting*. Chicago Linguistic Society, 1984.

[HW89] Berthold K. P. Horn and Patrick Henry Winston. *LISP*. Addison-Wesley, Reading, Mass, third edition, 1989.

[HW91] J. Hirschberg and G. Ward. The influence of pitch range, duration, amplitude, and spectral features on the interpretation of **l*+h l h%**. *Journal of Phonetics*, 1991.

[JSBG86] K. I. Joy, D. A. Sumikawa, M. M. Blattner, and R. M. Greenberg. Guidelines for the syntactic design of audio cues in computer interfaces. *Nineteenth Annual Hawaii International Conference on System Sciences*, 1986.

[Kat87] A. Katz. Issues in defining an equations representation standard. *ACM SIGSAM Bulletin*, 21(2):19–24, 1987.

[Kla87] Dennis H. Klatt. Review of text-to-speech conversion for English. *Acoustic Society of America Journal*, 82(3):737–783, September 1987.

[KLMN90] Pekka Kilpelainen, Greger Linden, Heikki Mannila, and Erja Nikunen. A structured document database system. In *Proceedings of the International Conference on Electronic Publishing, Document Manipulation & Typography*, pages 139–151. Cambridge University Press, September 1990.

[Knu84] Donald E. Knuth. *The TEXbook*. Addison-Wesley, Reading, Massachusetts, 1984.

[Knu86] Donald E. Knuth. *TEX The Program*. Addison-Wesley, Reading, Mass., 1986.

[KS84] Gary D. Kimura and Alan C. Shaw. The structure of abstract document objects. In *Proceedings of the Conference on Office Automation Systems*, Document Modeling and Management, pages 161–169. ACM, 1984.

[Lam86] Leslie Lamport. *LATEX: A Document Preparation System*. Addison-Wesley, Reading, Mass., 1986.

[LB87] A. Lippman and W. Bender. News and movies in the 50 megabit living room. *IEEE GlobeCom Proceedings*, (Tokyo, Japan, Nov. 1987).

[Lev88] David M. Levy. Topics in document research. In *ACM Conference on Document Processing Systems*, pages 187–193, December 5-9 1988. Santa Fe, New Mexico.

[LG90] Jose Valdeni De Lima and Henri Galy. The integration of structured documents into DBMS. In *Proceedings of the International Conference on Electronic Publishing, Document Manipulation & Typography*, pages 153–168. Cambridge University Press, 1990.

[LOS76] I. Lehiste, J. Olive, and L. Streeter. Role of duration in disambiguating syntactically ambiguous sentences. *Journal of the Acoustical Society of America*, 60:1199–1202, 1976.

[LPT+93] Thomas M. Levergood, Andrew C. Payne, G. Winfield Treese, James Gettys, and Lawrence C. Stewart. Audiofile: A network-transparent system for distributed audio applications. *Usenix*, 1993.

[ME92] Elizabeth D. Mynatt and W. Keith Edwards. Mapping GUIs to auditory interfaces. *Proceedings ACM UIST92*, pages 61–70, 1992.

[MOB90] S. A. Mamrak, C. S. O'Connell, and J. A. Barnes. The integrated chameleon architecture: A software toolset to support data translation. Technical Report OSU-CISRC-11/90-TR37, Department of Computer and Information Science, The Ohio State University, November 1990.

[OKDA73] M. M. O'Malley, D. Kloker, and B. Dara-Abrams. Recovering parentheses from spoken algebraic expressions. *IEEE Trans. Audio Electroacoust.*, AU-21:217–220, June 1973.

[Org90] International Standards Organization. *Information Technology: for Using SGML.* ISO/IEC, 1990.

[PH90] J. Pierrehumbert and J. Hirschberg. The meaning of intonational contours in the interpretation of discourse. In *Intentions in Communication.* MIT Press, Cambridge MA, 1990.

[PI88] W. Timothy Polk and Lawrence E. Bassham III. A window and icon based prototype for expert assistance for manipulation of SGML document type definitions. In *ACM Conference on Document Processing Systems*, Document Standards, pages 79–84. ACM, 1988.

[Pie81] Janet Pierrehumbert. Synthesizing intonation. *Journal of the Acoustical Society of America*, 70(4):985–995, October 1981.

[PR92] Gilbert B. Porter and Emil V. Rainero. Document reconstruction: A system for recovering document structure for layout. *Electronic Publishing*, 1992.

[PS88] Lynne A. Price and Joe Schneider. Evolution of an SGML application generator. In *ACM Conference on Document Processing Systems*, Experience with Document Standards, pages 51–60. ACM, 1988.

[QNA90] Vincent Quint, Marc Nanard, and Jacques Andre. Towards document engineering. In *Proceedings of the International Conference on Electronic Publishing, Document Manipulation & Typography*, pages 17–29. Cambridge University Press, September 1990.

[QV92] Vincent Quint and Irene Vatton. Combining hypertext and structured documents in grif. In *Proceedings of the Fourth ACM Conference on Hypertext*, Systems I, pages 23–32. ACM, 1992.

[Ram89] T. V. Raman. CONGRATS: Converting graphics to sound. Master's thesis, Indian Institute of Technology, Bombay, May 1989. Masters thesis report.

[Ram91] T. V. Raman. TEXTALK. *TUGboat*, 12:178, March 1991.

[Ram92] T. V. Raman. An audio view of (LA)TEX documents. *Proceedings of the TEX Users Group*, 13:372–379, July 1992.

[Ram96a] T. V. Raman. Emacspeak —direct speech access. *Proc. of The Second Annual ACM Conference on Assistive Technologies (ASSETS '96)*, Apr 1996.

[Ram96b] T.Ṽ. Raman. Emacspeak –a speech interface. *Proceedings of CHI96*, April 1996.

[Ram97a] T. V. Raman. *Auditory User Interfaces –Toward The Speaking Computer.* Kluwer Academic Publishers, August 1997.

[Ram97b] T. V. Raman. Net surfing without a monitor. *Scientific American*, March 1997.

[Res92] Paul Resnick. *HyperVoice: Groupware by Telephone.* PhD thesis, MIT, 1992.

[RK92] T. V. Raman and M. S. Krishnamoorthy. Congrats: A system for converting graphics to sound. *Proceedings of IEEE on Johns Hopkins National Search for Computing Applications to Assist Persons with Disabilities*, pages 170–172, February 1992.

[RT84] T. Reps and T. Teitelbaum. The synthesizer generator. *Proceedings of the ACM SIGSOFT/SIGPLAN Software Engineering Symposium on Practical Software Development Environments*, pages 42–48, 1984.

[RT88a] T. Reps and T. Teitelbaum. *The Synthesizer Generator: A System for Constructing Language-Based Editors.* Springer-Verlag, NY, 1988.

[RT88b] T. Reps and T. Teitelbaum. *The Synthesizer Generator Reference Manual.* Springer-Verlag, Third edition, 1988. First edition, Cornell University, August, 1985; Second edition, Cornell University, June, 1987.

[RW85] S. Roucos and A. M. Wilgus. High quality time-scale modification for speech. *Proceedings of the International Conference on Acoustics, Speech and Signal Processing*, pages 493–496, 1985.

[SA89] C. Schmandt and B. Arons. Getting the word (desktop audio). *Unix Review*, 7:54–62, October 1989.

[SASH93] L. J. Stifelman, B. Arons, C. Schmandt, and Eric Hulteen. Voicenotes: A speech interface for a hand-held voice notetaker. *Proceedings of INTERCHI Conference, ACM SIGCHI*, 1993.

[SB92] Manojit Sarkar and Mark H. Brown. Graphical fish eye views of graphs. *Technical Report*, March 1992.

[SF88] P. David Stotts and Richard Furuta. Adding browsing semantics to the hypertext model. In *ACM Conference on Document Processing Systems*, Hypertext, pages 43–50. ACM, 1988.

[SF90] P. David Stotts and Richard Furuta. Hierarchy, composition, scripting languages, and translators for structured hypertext. In *Proceedings of the ECHT'90 European Conference on Hypertext*, Turning Text into Hypertext, pages 180–193. Cambridge University Press, 1990.

[SFR92] P. David Stotts, Richard Furuta, and J. Cyrano Ruiz. Hyperdocuments as automata: Trace-based browsing property verification. In *Proceedings of the Fourth ACM Conference on Hypertext*, Architecture, pages 272–281. ACM, 1992.

[SGM86] International Organization for Standardization. *Information Processing: Text and Office Systems: Standard Generalized Markup Language SGML*, October 1986. ISO 8879-1986 E.

[SMG90] D. A. Sumikawa, Blattner M. M., and R. M. Greenberg. Earcons and icons: Their structure and common design principles. *Visual Programming Environments*, 1990.

[Ste90] Guy L. Steele. *Common Lisp The Language.* Digital Press, Bedford, Mass, second edition, 1990.

[Str78] Lynn Streeter. Acoustic determinants of phrase boundary perception. *Acoustics Society of America, Journal*, 64(6):1582–1592, 1978.

[Tec91] Institute On Applied Technology. *MultiVoice 1.0 —Owner's and Programmer's Manual.* Institute On Applied Technology, 300 Longwood Avenue, Boston, MA 02115, 1991. The MultiVoice is based on Dectalk 3.0.

[Ver90] Anne-Marie Vercoustre. Structured editing - hypertext approach: Cooperation and complementarity. In *Proceedings of the International Conference on Electronic Publishing, Document Manipulation & Typography*, pages 65–78. Cambridge University Press, September 1990.

[WF90] Elizabeth M. Wenzel and Scott H. Foster. Real time digital synthesis of virtual acoustic environments. *Computer Graphics, Special Issue on 1990 symposium on interactive 3d graphics*, 24.2, March 1990.

[WH91] Michelle Q. Wang and Julia Hirschberg. Predicting intonational boundaries automatically from text: The ATIS domain. In *Proceedings.* DARPA Speech and Natural Language Workshop, February 1991.

[WWK91] Elizabeth M. Wenzel, Fredric L. Wightman, and Doris J. Kistler. Localization with non-individualized virtual acoustic display cues. *Proceedings of the ACM*, 1991.

[X3J93] Accredited Standards Committee X3J13. *Programming Language —Common Lisp— Draft Proposed.* CBEMA, 1993. *URL* FTP://parcftp.xerox.com/pub/cl/dpANS2.

[Yel88] Daniel M. Yellin. *Attribute Grammar Inversion and Source-To-Source Translation.* Springer-Verlag, Berlin, New York, 1988.

[ZP86] Ingrid Zuckerman and Judea Pearl. Comprehension-driven generation of meta-technical utterances in math tutoring. In *Proceedings of the Fifth National Conference*, pages 606–611, Philadelphia, 1986. AAAI.

Lecture Notes in Computer Science

For information about Vols. 1–1469
please contact your bookseller or Springer-Verlag

Vol. 1470: D. Pritchard, J. Reeve (Eds.), Euro-Par'98: Parallel Processing. Proceedings, 1998. XXII, 1157 pages. 1998.

Vol. 1471: J. Dix, L. Moniz Pereira, T.C. Przymusinski (Eds.), Logic Programming and Knowledge Representation. Proceedings, 1997. IX, 246 pages. 1998. (Subseries LNAI).

Vol. 1472: B. Freitag, H. Decker, M. Kifer, A. Voronkov (Eds.), Transactions and Change in Logic Databases. Proceedings, 1996, 1997. X, 396 pages. 1998.

Vol. 1473: X. Leroy, A. Ohori (Eds.), Types in Compilation. Proceedings, 1998. VIII, 299 pages. 1998.

Vol. 1474: F. Mueller, A. Bestavros (Eds.), Languages, Compilers, and Tools for Embedded Systems. Proceedings, 1998. XIV, 261 pages. 1998.

Vol. 1475: W. Litwin, T. Morzy, G. Vossen (Eds.), Advances in Databases and Information Systems. Proceedings, 1998. XIV, 369 pages. 1998.

Vol. 1476: J. Calmet, J. Plaza (Eds.), Artificial Intelligence and Symbolic Computation. Proceedings, 1998. XI, 309 pages. 1998. (Subseries LNAI).

Vol. 1477: K. Rothermel, F. Hohl (Eds.), Mobile Agents. Proceedings, 1998. VIII, 285 pages. 1998.

Vol. 1478: M. Sipper, D. Mange, A. Pérez-Uribe (Eds.), Evolvable Systems: From Biology to Hardware. Proceedings, 1998. IX, 382 pages. 1998.

Vol. 1479: J. Grundy, M. Newey (Eds.), Theorem Proving in Higher Order Logics. Proceedings, 1998. VIII, 497 pages. 1998.

Vol. 1480: F. Giunchiglia (Ed.), Artificial Intelligence: Methodology, Systems, and Applications. Proceedings, 1998. IX, 502 pages. 1998. (Subseries LNAI).

Vol. 1481: E.V. Munson, C. Nicholas, D. Wood (Eds.), Principles of Digital Document Processing. Proceedings, 1998. VII, 152 pages. 1998.

Vol. 1482: R.W. Hartenstein, A. Keevallik (Eds.), Field-Programmable Logic and Applications. Proceedings, 1998. XI, 533 pages. 1998.

Vol. 1483: T. Plagemann, V. Goebel (Eds.), Interactive Distributed Multimedia Systems and Telecommunication Services. Proceedings, 1998. XV, 326 pages. 1998.

Vol. 1484: H. Coelho (Ed.), Progress in Artificial Intelligence – IBERAMIA 98. Proceedings, 1998. XIII, 421 pages. 1998. (Subseries LNAI).

Vol. 1485: J.-J. Quisquater, Y. Deswarte, C. Meadows, D. Gollmann (Eds.), Computer Security – ESORICS 98. Proceedings, 1998. X, 377 pages. 1998.

Vol. 1486: A.P. Ravn, H. Rischel (Eds.), Formal Techniques in Real-Time and Fault-Tolerant Systems. Proceedings, 1998. VIII, 339 pages. 1998.

Vol. 1487: V. Gruhn (Ed.), Software Process Technology. Proceedings, 1998. VIII, 157 pages. 1998.

Vol. 1488: B. Smyth, P. Cunningham (Eds.), Advances in Case-Based Reasoning. Proceedings, 1998. XI, 482 pages. 1998. (Subseries LNAI).

Vol. 1489: J. Dix, L. Fariñas del Cerro, U. Furbach (Eds.), Logics in Artificial Intelligence. Proceedings, 1998. X, 391 pages. 1998. (Subseries LNAI).

Vol. 1490: C. Palamidessi, H. Glaser, K. Meinke (Eds.), Principles of Declarative Programming. Proceedings, 1998. XI, 497 pages. 1998.

Vol. 1491: W. Reisig, G. Rozenberg (Eds.), Lectures on Petri Nets I: Basic Models. XII, 683 pages. 1998.

Vol. 1492: W. Reisig, G. Rozenberg (Eds.), Lectures on Petri Nets II: Applications. XII, 479 pages. 1998.

Vol. 1493: J.P. Bowen, A. Fett, M.G. Hinchey (Eds.), ZUM '98: The Z Formal Specification Notation. Proceedings, 1998. XV, 417 pages. 1998.

Vol. 1494: G. Rozenberg, F. Vaandrager (Eds.), Lectures on Embedded Systems. Proceedings, 1996. VIII, 423 pages. 1998.

Vol. 1495: T. Andreasen, H. Christiansen, H.L. Larsen (Eds.), Flexible Query Answering Systems. IX, 393 pages. 1998. (Subseries LNAI).

Vol. 1496: W.M. Wells, A. Colchester, S. Delp (Eds.), Medical Image Computing and Computer-Assisted Intervention – MICCAI'98. Proceedings, 1998. XXII, 1256 pages. 1998.

Vol. 1497: V. Alexandrov, J. Dongarra (Eds.), Recent Advances in Parallel Virtual Machine and Message Passing Interface. Proceedings, 1998. XII, 412 pages. 1998.

Vol. 1498: A.E. Eiben, T. Bäck, M. Schoenauer, H.-P. Schwefel (Eds.), Parallel Problem Solving from Nature – PPSN V. Proceedings, 1998. XXIII, 1041 pages. 1998.

Vol. 1499: S. Kutten (Ed.), Distributed Computing. Proceedings, 1998. XII, 419 pages. 1998.

Vol. 1501: M.M. Richter, C.H. Smith, R. Wiehagen, T. Zeugmann (Eds.), Algorithmic Learning Theory. Proceedings, 1998. XI, 439 pages. 1998. (Subseries LNAI).

Vol. 1502: G. Antoniou, J. Slaney (Eds.), Advanced Topics in Artificial Intelligence. Proceedings, 1998. XI, 333 pages. 1998. (Subseries LNAI).

Vol. 1503: G. Levi (Ed.), Static Analysis. Proceedings, 1998. IX, 383 pages. 1998.

Vol. 1504: O. Herzog, A. Günter (Eds.), KI-98: Advances in Artificial Intelligence. Proceedings, 1998. XI, 355 pages. 1998. (Subseries LNAI).

Vol. 1505: D. Caromel, R.R. Oldehoeft, M. Tholburn (Eds.), Computing in Object-Oriented Parallel Environments. Proceedings, 1998. XI, 243 pages. 1998.

Vol. 1506: R. Koch, L. Van Gool (Eds.), 3D Structure from Multiple Images of Large-Scale Environments. Proceedings, 1998. VIII, 347 pages. 1998.

Vol. 1507: T.W. Ling, S. Ram, M.L. Lee (Eds.), Conceptual Modeling – ER '98. Proceedings, 1998. XVI, 482 pages. 1998.

Vol. 1508: S. Jajodia, M.T. Özsu, A. Dogac (Eds.), Advances in Multimedia Information Systems. Proceedings, 1998. VIII, 207 pages. 1998.

Vol. 1510: J.M. Zytkow, M. Quafafou (Eds.), Principles of Data Mining and Knowledge Discovery. Proceedings, 1998. XI, 482 pages. 1998. (Subseries LNAI).

Vol. 1511: D. O'Hallaron (Ed.), Languages, Compilers, and Run-Time Systems for Scalable Computers. Proceedings, 1998. IX, 412 pages. 1998.

Vol. 1512: E. Giménez, C. Paulin-Mohring (Eds.), Types for Proofs and Programs. Proceedings, 1996. VIII, 373 pages. 1998.

Vol. 1513: C. Nikolaou, C. Stephanidis (Eds.), Research and Advanced Technology for Digital Libraries. Proceedings, 1998. XV, 912 pages. 1998.

Vol. 1514: K. Ohta, D. Pei (Eds.), Advances in Cryptology – ASIACRYPT'98. Proceedings, 1998. XII, 436 pages. 1998.

Vol. 1515: F. Moreira de Oliveira (Ed.), Advances in Artificial Intelligence. Proceedings, 1998. X, 259 pages. 1998. (Subseries LNAI).

Vol. 1516: W. Ehrenberger (Ed.), Computer Safety, Reliability and Security. Proceedings, 1998. XVI, 392 pages. 1998.

Vol. 1517: J. Hromkovič, O. Sýkora (Eds.), Graph-Theoretic Concepts in Computer Science. Proceedings, 1998. X, 385 pages. 1998.

Vol. 1518: M. Luby, J. Rolim, M. Serna (Eds.), Randomization and Approximation Techniques in Computer Science. Proceedings, 1998. IX, 385 pages. 1998.

1519: T. Ishida (Ed.), Community Computing and Support Systems. VIII, 393 pages. 1998.

Vol. 1520: M. Maher, J.-F. Puget (Eds.), Principles and Practice of Constraint Programming - CP98. Proceedings, 1998. XI, 482 pages. 1998.

Vol. 1521: B. Rovan (Ed.), SOFSEM'98: Theory and Practice of Informatics. Proceedings, 1998. XI, 453 pages. 1998.

Vol. 1522: G. Gopalakrishnan, P. Windley (Eds.), Formal Methods in Computer-Aided Design. Proceedings, 1998. IX, 529 pages. 1998.

Vol. 1524: G.B. Orr, K.-R. Müller (Eds.), Neural Networks: Tricks of the Trade. VI, 432 pages. 1998.

Vol. 1525: D. Aucsmith (Ed.), Information Hiding. Proceedings, 1998. IX, 369 pages. 1998.

Vol. 1526: M. Broy, B. Rumpe (Eds.), Requirements Targeting Software and Systems Engineering. Proceedings, 1997. VIII, 357 pages. 1998.

Vol. 1527: P. Baumgartner, Theory Reasoning in Connection Calculi. IX, 283. 1999. (Subseries LNAI).

Vol. 1528: B. Preneel, V. Rijmen (Eds.), State of the Art in Applied Cryptography. Revised Lectures, 1997. VIII, 395 pages. 1998.

Vol. 1529: D. Farwell, L. Gerber, E. Hovy (Eds.), Machine Translation and the Information Soup. Proceedings, 1998. XIX, 532 pages. 1998. (Subseries LNAI).

Vol. 1530: V. Arvind, R. Ramanujam (Eds.), Foundations of Software Technology and Theoretical Computer Science. XII, 369 pages. 1998.

Vol. 1531: H.-Y. Lee, H. Motoda (Eds.), PRICAI'98: Topics in Artificial Intelligence. XIX, 646 pages. 1998. (Subseries LNAI).

Vol. 1096: T. Schael, Workflow Management Systems for Process Organisations. Second Edition. XII, 229 pages. 1998.

Vol. 1532: S. Arikawa, H. Motoda (Eds.), Discovery Science. Proceedings, 1998. XI, 456 pages. 1998. (Subseries LNAI).

Vol. 1533: K.-Y. Chwa, O.H. Ibarra (Eds.), Algorithms and Computation. Proceedings, 1998. XIII, 478 pages. 1998.

Vol. 1534: J.S. Sichman, R. Conte, N. Gilbert (Eds.), Multi-Agent Systems and Agent-Based Simulation. Proceedings, 1998. VIII, 237 pages. 1998. (Subseries LNAI).

Vol. 1535: S. Ossowski, Co-ordination in Artificial Agent Societies. XV; 221 pages. 1999. (Subseries LNAI).

Vol. 1536: W.-P. de Roever, H. Langmaack, A. Pnueli (Eds.), Compositionality: The Significant Difference. Proceedings, 1997. VIII, 647 pages. 1998.

Vol. 1538: J. Hsiang, A. Ohori (Eds.), Advances in Computing Science – ASIAN'98. Proceedings, 1998. X, 305 pages. 1998.

Vol. 1539: O. Rüthing, Interacting Code Motion Transformations: Their Impact and Their Complexity. XXI,225 pages. 1999.

Vol. 1540: C. Beeri, P. Buneman (Eds.), Database Theory – ICDT'99. Proceedings, 1999. XI, 489 pages. 1999.

Vol. 1541: B. Kågström, J. Dongarra, E. Elmroth, J. Waśniewski (Eds.), Applied Parallel Computing. Proceedings, 1998. XIV, 586 pages. 1998.

Vol. 1542: H.I. Christensen (Ed.), Computer Vision Systems. Proceedings, 1999. XI, 554 pages. 1999.

Vol. 1543: S. Demeyer, J. Bosch (Eds.), Object-Oriented Technology ECOOP'98 Workshop Reader. 1998. XXII, 573 pages. 1998.

Vol. 1544: C. Zhang, D. Lukose (Eds.), Multi-Agent Systems. Proceedings, 1998. VII, 195 pages. 1998. (Subseries LNAI).

Vol. 1545: A. Birk, J. Demiris (Eds.), Learning Robots. Proceedings, 1996. IX, 188 pages. 1998. (Subseries LNAI).

Vol. 1546: B. Möller, J.V. Tucker (Eds.), Prospects for Hardware Foundations. Survey Chapters, 1998. X, 468 pages. 1998.

Vol. 1547: S. H. Whitesides (Ed.), Graph Drawing. Proceedings 1998. XII, 468 pages. 1998.

Vol. 1548: A.M. Haeberer (Ed.), Algebraic Methodology and Software Technology. Proceedings, 1999. XI, 531 pages. 1999.

Vol. 1551: G. Gupta (Ed.), Practical Aspects of Declarative Languages. Proceedings, 1999. VIII, 367 pgages. 1999.